The Basics Of SCRUM

ADITI AGARWAL

Published By: Aditi Agarwal Books LLC
Date of Publication: May 2017
Language: English

FREE Membership to Project Management Mentoring Network

Be a mentor, or learn from experienced Project Managers by subscribing to the exclusive Project Management Facebook Network for Free:

https://www.facebook.com/groups/ProjectManagementMentoringNetwork/

To my family for their loving support

Table of Contents

Introduction

Today, in corporate world, everyone is talking about Scrum. Major companies like Amazon, Google, Microsoft, IBM, Deloitte, American Express, and many more have adopted Scrum concepts. This book is written to provide a simplified handbook to you such that you can familiarize yourself with the most popular Agile process framework to build complex software products.

Who Should Read This Book?
-   Experienced Project Managers
-   Aspiring Project Managers
-   Business Analysts
-   Developers or Programmers
-   Test Managers and Engineers
-   Business Project Managers or Leads
-   Business and Technical Leaders
-   Subject Matter Experts
-   Students seeking an IT job
-   Anyone who needs to learn the most popular Agile framework to expand one's career opportunities.

- Anyone who needs a short and simple reference book on Scrum.
- Anyone who doesn't have time to read large detailed books on Scrum.
- Anyone who needs to understand Scrum before enrolling into a training or a certification course.

Why Did I Write This Book?

As a Scrum Master, I am continuously looking for books on Scrum. I have read detailed guides and large books on Scrum. I have also seen books that cover various agile methodologies. But, I have not been able to find a concise handbook that can explain the complete Scrum framework to busy professionals. This book is an attempt to fill the missing gap between a 500-page detailed Scrum guide and a one-pager blog. I wrote this book so that you can learn Scrum at any place and any time you want – whether you are travelling, eating at cafeteria, need a handy reference on your desk, need to coach new team members, attending long meetings (though I recommend that you pay attention in the meetings), waiting for your appointment etc. I hope this book will serve as a good starting point on your journey to learn Scrum.

How to Use This Book?

If you are new to Scrum, I expect that you read this book from front to back. For those who are more familiar with Scrum, you can use this book as a reference guide or a handbook. If you are interested to learn about Scrum roles and responsibilities, jump to Chapter 3. If you are more interested in understanding the differences between traditional approach and Scrum approach, I highly recommend that you read Chapter 2 – Why Scrum? and Chapter 6 – Agile Principles. If you are rather interested in understanding more about technical debt, you can switch to Chapter 9 – Technical Debt.

Ready, Set, Go

Set aside some time during the day to read and know Scrum. The chapters that follow describe the most widely used framework to build and deliver complex products. Happy Reading!

Acknowledgements

First, I would like to express my gratitude to God whose blessings gave me an inspiration to write this book. I strongly believe in sharing my knowledge and helping others to succeed.

I would like to acknowledge the support of my parents who have always believed in me. Their unconditional love give me the courage to move forward.

This book would not have been possible without the support of my husband. I will take this opportunity to thank him for his continued support and encouragement.

Then, a special thanks to my son whose curious questions inspired me to share my knowledge and teach a complex subject in a simple manner.

I also thank my colleagues, my friends, and my mentors who trust my abilities and knowledge to write this book.

I'd also like to thank the people who took time out from their busy schedules to review chapters and send me their feedback.

Chapter 1 – What is Scrum?

What Is Scrum?

Scrum is a basic structure or a set of guidelines defined to build and deliver valuable products. It is widely defined as an iterative or incremental process framework to build complex products of highest possible value.

Scrum originally was formalized for software development projects, but it works well for any complex and innovative piece of work. It is lightweight and simple to understand. The Scrum process framework consists of a Scrum team and their associated roles, along with Scrum artifacts, ceremonies, principles, rules, and communication charts.

Scrum is an incremental approach to develop a product through successive improvements. Using Scrum, small improvements are made to the product in pieces, also known as product increments. The first product increment will have only few features of the product. With subsequent iterations, the product gets refined and more features are added to the product.

The first product increment is commonly called MVP (Minimum Viable Product). This is a product increment with just enough features that make it usable and viable. The purpose of a MVP is to seek early feedback from the customer and adapt based on the feedback.

I like to quote this analogy to explain the benefits of an incremental approach and a Minimum Viable Product. Assume that a customer needs a newly designed car. A Scrum team gets formed who delivers a skateboard as the Minimum Viable Product to the customer at the end of their first iteration. Though a skateboard is not the final product desired by the customer, it still gives value to the customer and enables the team to seek customer feedback. Next, the Scrum team refines the skateboard and delivers a bicycle to the customer at the end of their next iteration. This again is not the desired final product, but nonetheless, provides value to the customer. The team, again, refines their product, add more features into it, and deliver a bike to the customer at the end of their next iteration. The customer stays happy as he continues to see the team's progress and receive a valuable product at the end of each iteration. Finally, the team adds more features to their product and delivers a car to the customer. In this approach, the team develops the final product through continuous refinement and delivers value at the end of each iteration. On the other hand, when the same product is created with a plan-driven traditional development approach, the customer does not see any real value till the end of the project. Often, the requirements of the customer do not match the delivered product, and the customer stays unsatisfied.

In Scrum, the team always work on the highest priority items first. The work is performed in short, time boxed iterations. Each iteration begins when the team aligns on a subset of the highest priority items that it can complete in that iteration. Each iteration ends when the team has delivered a potentially shippable product increment of the product. The team delivers value to the customer at the end of each iteration or a time boxed cycle.

Let's take a simple case study to understand the key differences between traditional development and Scrum development methodologies.

A Case Study

An entrepreneur assigns two separate teams to create a new website for his business. Team A seeks clarification and gathers requirements for all the required features on the website, and then starts designing the same. Team B, on the other hand, asks the entrepreneur to rank the different features of the website in a priority order and decides to follow an iterative approach by focusing only on the highest priority items first.

Team A follows a sequential method to develop the website, widely known as 'Waterfall' or traditional method. In this model, analyze phase starts only when define phase is complete, design phase starts when analyze phase is complete, build phase starts when design phase is complete, and so on. One can move to a next phase only when it's preceding phase is reviewed and approved by all key stakeholders.

In Waterfall method, the progress flows steadily downwards like a waterfall (see Fig 1). The common phases are: Define, Analyze, Design, Build, Test, Launch, and Maintain. The rule is that the preceding phase must be completed before the next phase can begin.

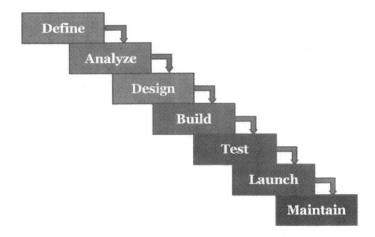

Fig. 1: Traditional or Waterfall approach

Team A followed the Waterfall approach as they gathered all the requirements first, then verified the completeness of the requirements with the entrepreneur, before starting to design the website. Once their design was completed, they again verified the same with the entrepreneur before starting to build the site.

Team B, on the other hand, followed an iterative approach (see Fig 2) to build the website incrementally, instead of trying to build it all at once. The team analyzed, designed, developed, and tested the highest priority feature first. This approach is widely known as 'Agile Development', in which work evolve through collaboration between self-organizing and cross-functional teams. This approach promotes adaptive planning, iterative development, early delivery, continuous improvement, and encourages rapid and flexible response to change.

The word 'Agile' means being 'able to move quickly and easily'. Scrum is one of the most popular Agile methodologies used to develop complex products in an iterative manner. This approach supports faster time to market and shorter development cycles.

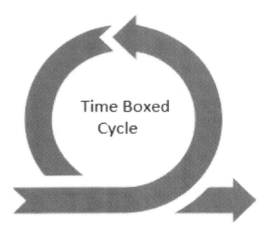

Fig. 2: Iterative approach

In this approach, the team works in time-boxed cycles known as Sprints or iterations, and move from analyze to test or rollout phases within each iteration for the prioritized piece of the work.

Origins of Scrum

In the early 1990s, Ken Schwaber and Jeff Sutherland conceived the Scrum process. In 1995, they jointly presented a paper describing the Scrum methodology at the Oopsla conference in Austin, Texas.

Ken and Jeff inherited the name 'Scrum' from the 1986 paper 'The New New Product

Development Game' by Takeuchi and Nonaka, two famous management thinkers. With the term 'Scrum', they wanted to stress the importance of teams and highlight some analogies between a team sport like rugby and the new game of product development. In rugby football, a Scrum refers to a tight packed formation of players with their heads down who attempt to gain possession of the ball. Scrum is often called the rugby approach.

Scrum is a leading Agile development methodology, used by Fortune 500 companies around the world. It is the solid and proven framework that has been applied to a variety of products and teams.

Summary

Scrum is an iterative and incremental development approach used to build complex products. In the next chapter, I will focus on the benefits of Scrum. I will also compare Scrum development approach with traditional plan-driven approach, so you can decide which approach works best in your situation.

Chapter 2 – Why Scrum?

This chapter describes the need for Scrum and its benefits, as compared to the traditional plan-driven development approach. It also emphasizes when and when not to use Scrum.

Need for Scrum

While the traditional development approach worked well earlier, but the growing need for rapid exploration and feedback did not mesh well with the detailed upfront planning that we had been doing.

With Waterfall approach, there was a lot of mismatch between the requirements and the final product. Often, the end user of the product was unhappy with the final product, and the development team failed to understand the reason of his or her dis-satisfaction despite their hard work throughout the development process.

Think about the website development case study. Team A, who followed the Waterfall approach, developed the website in three months after receiving the sign-off or the entrepreneur's approval on the requirements, layout, and the technical design. It is highly likely that when they finally completed their development, the website did not meet all the requirements. Or, it may happen that the entrepreneur desired new features on the website, or suggested a revised layout during the test phase. In such scenarios, Team A will need to go back to the drawing board, gather the requirements again, revisit their technical and front end design, and re-build the website!

Scrum, on the other hand, is based on shorter development cycles of 2-4 weeks called the 'Sprints' that allow the sponsors (also known as 'business' in some corporations) and other stakeholders to review the incremental work done by the team in each Sprint. This narrows the mismatch between the business expectations and the delivered product. Scrum enables frequent communication and alignment with the stakeholders.

Team B who followed an iterative approach provided live demonstrations to the entrepreneur every two weeks and incorporated changes as requested by him. The entrepreneur got an opportunity to review their work at the end of every Sprint. Team B continued to build the required features for the website in accordance with the priorities defined by the entrepreneur. Thus, they completed their development in much shorter timeframe. By following an iterative approach, Team B always stayed focused and met the changing needs of the entrepreneur.

Benefits of Scrum

Scrum was developed to solve the below problems with the traditional plan-driven development method:

- Long development cycles
- Mismatch between requirements and actual product implementation
- De-motivated team members
- Unhappy customers
- Late customer feedback and late learning
- Huge rework and high cost of change

In our case study, assume that when Team A completed the development and handed it over to the entrepreneur for testing, the entrepreneur asked them to add new features to the website and change the front-end layout of the application. Such changes during the test phase lead to a lot of re-work, resulting in increased cost, delayed time to market, and overall dissatisfaction.

This happens very often in software development projects. The requirements change during the long development cycle due to various reasons such as changed market conditions, new technology, increased competition, etc.

Team B, on the other hand, worked very closely with the entrepreneur to prioritize the requirements, which means listing down the high-level features in a priority order. Team B then built the most prioritized feature within the next two weeks and provided a demonstration of their completed work to the entrepreneur at the end of their two-week Sprint. The entrepreneur gave feedback for the completed work, provided details for the next priority feature, changed the priority of features in the work list, and even deleted features, as needed. In this approach, the entrepreneur had an opportunity to review the website development every two weeks and provide feedback.

By following an iterative approach, Team B could adapt to changes, narrow down any mismatch between the customer expectations and the final product, keep the customer happy, and stay motivated.

Scrum is well suited to help organizations succeed in a complex world where they must quickly adapt to stay ahead of competition and delight their customers.

With traditional plan-based development approach, customer feedback is given a long time after development during the test phase. The team designs and builds the system based on initial assumptions and then waits to validate their assumptions in the test phase. Late customer feedback results in late learning and expensive rework. In this approach, most of the learning happens at the end of the project. The team documents their lessons learnt and leverages their learning only in the next project.

Scrum, on the other hand, enables fast customer feedback and constant learning. There are predefined inspect and adapt activities such as Daily Scrum, Sprint Review, and Sprint Retrospective ceremonies that allow fast feedback and constant learning. I will describe Scrum ceremonies in subsequent chapters.

When to use Scrum

It is important to understand when and when not to use Scrum. Though Scrum is an excellent framework for several projects, it may not be the appropriate solution for all projects. Most of the efforts fall into these domains – complex, complicated, simple, and chaotic.

Scrum is most suited for complex projects where things are more unpredictable than they are predictable. In complex domains, there is a need to collaborate with others, have an innovative mindset to investigate, experiment different ideas, and adapt based on the learnings. New product development and enhancement of an existing product with new innovative features are some examples of a complex effort.

In complicated domains, things are more predictable than they are unpredictable. In such situations, there is a need to assess multiple options and select the best option based on best practices or past experiences. Scrum may be applied in such scenarios; however, it may not be the best approach. A well-defined quantitative approach may be better suited for such efforts. Few examples of complicated efforts are increasing application availability, improving system performance, product maintenance, and improving the quality of a product.

For simple projects, things are predictable and stable. The solution is obvious and known. The best practices are established. Scrum may be applied for such domains; however, it may not be the best approach. A step-by-step defined process may be better suited for such efforts. Configuration changes, product or software installations, infrastructure updates etc. are some examples of simple efforts.

Scrum is not suited for chaotic efforts. In chaotic conditions, we need to act immediately to re-establish order and stability. There are no clear solutions in such conditions. There is no time to prioritize the activities. A production outage that leads to revenue loss, or a legal issue with potential to result in brand damage are examples of chaotic efforts.

Scrum is best suited for complex product development efforts. By using Scrum, you'll become more Agile, discovering how to react more quickly and respond more accurately to the inevitable change that comes your way. So, whether you're working on the next smartphone app, new website, or development of new features for your product, you should take a closer look at using Scrum.

Summary

This chapter emphasized the need for Scrum framework and described the benefits of Scrum in comparison to the traditional plan-driven development approach. In this chapter, I also described the different types of efforts to help you decide when and when not to use Scrum. In the next chapter, I will explain Scrum roles.

Chapter 3 – Scrum Roles

In this chapter, let's learn about different roles in a Scrum Team. A Scrum Team consists of three roles: Product Owner, Scrum Master, and the Development Team (see Fig. 3).

A Product Owner decides what needs to be built and in what order. A Scrum Master acts as a servant leader and coaches the team to follow Agile Scrum principles. A Development Team is a group of self-organizing individuals who develop a high-quality product.

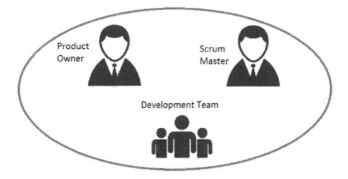

Fig. 3: Different Scrum roles

A. Product Owner

A Product Owner is responsible for what will be developed and in what order. He owns the success of the product being developed.

He represents the business (or the project sponsor), acts as a liaison between the development team and customers, and collaborates closely with both groups to ensure there is a clear understanding of what features are needed in the product.

In our case study of website development, who do you think was the Product Owner? The entrepreneur acted as the Product Owner to Team B, as he instructed what needs to be created and in what order.

Let's look at the responsibilities of a Product Owner. A Product Owner is a primary stakeholder who is responsible to have a vision for the product. He is either the primary user of the product or has a solid understanding of the user's needs. He knows the market trends, competitor's strengths, and creates a product roadmap. He tries his best to build the best product possible. He is also a strong communicator who manages the expectations of other stakeholders.

Responsibilities of a Product Owner

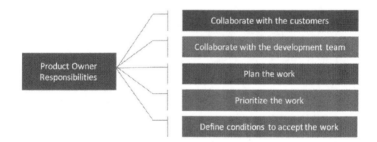

Fig. 4: Responsibilities of a Product Owner

Collaborate with the customers

A Product Owner is the single point of contact for all interested parties including customers, partners, leadership, executives, and others. He collaborates with other stakeholders and manages their expectations for the product. He communicates the product strategy to the senior leadership and balances the demands of the stakeholders. A Product Owner is responsible to communicate the product priorities to the stakeholders and gain their alignment.

Collaborate with the Development Team

A Product Owner works very closely with the Development Team every day. He translates his product vision and priorities to requirements or User Stories. He also collaborates with the Scrum Master and prioritizes product requirements or User Stories to be worked upon by the Development Team.

In Waterfall or traditional method, the project sponsor (one who funds the project) engages with the development team only at the beginning to define the complete set of requirements and then re-engages only at the near end to perform user acceptance testing (to inspect and accept the work). The level of customer engagement is very low in this approach.

On the other hand, with Scrum, the level of engagement between the Product Owner and the Development Team is very high. The Product Owner prioritizes the requirements or User Stories, collaborates with the Development Team to estimate the complexity and the required effort, and provides regular feedback.

He always stays on top of the work being done by the Development Team. He is easily available to answer any questions from the development team. His close interaction and strong relationship with the Development Team is very essential to a successful product release.

Plan the Work

The Product Owner works very closely with the stakeholders to create a goal or business objectives for the product. He creates a product roadmap and defines the product priorities in alignment with the product strategy and business objectives.

The Product Owner plans the work to be done by the Development Team. He prioritizes the requirements or User Stories, understands the velocity of the Scrum team, and continually accepts the work or User Stories during the Sprint.

Prioritize the Work

The Product Owner decides what needs to be done and in what order. He creates a list of features, also called a Product Backlog, which aligns with the business objectives and the aligned roadmap for the product. He, then, prioritizes the same in accordance with the product priorities.

He also grooms the top few prioritized features on the Product Backlog such that the Development Team can estimate the required effort to develop the same.

Define conditions to accept the work

The Product Owner defines the acceptance criteria for each requirement or feature in the Product Backlog. This is the criteria or conditions that must be met for the work to be accepted by the Product Owner.

The acceptance conditions are very critical to ensure a quality product. The Product Owner works closely with the Scrum Master and the Development Team to define the acceptance criteria and gain alignment on the same.

B. Scrum Master

The Scrum Master helps everyone to understand and follow the Scrum values, principles, and practices. He acts as a coach to the Scrum team. The Scrum Master is also responsible to resolve any issues or impediments for the Development Team. He facilitates various Scrum ceremonies and ensures that the progress made by the Development Team is transparent to the key stakeholders at any time. He ensures that the Agile maturity of the team increases with time.

In our earlier case study of website development, assume that a person gets assigned to provide his guidance to Team B. He works very closely with the entrepreneur and assists him to prioritize the list of features required for the website. He guides the team to meet every day and discuss their progress with each other. He facilitates the website product demonstration with the entrepreneur at the end of every two-week Sprint. He also ensures that Team B does not have any impediments to proceed further with their development. He works closely with the entrepreneur to define the acceptance criteria for the required features on the website. He also shields Team B from any outside interference such that they can focus on delivering value at the end of every two-week iteration or Sprint. In this example, this person acts as a Scrum Master for Team B.

A Scrum Master is a key role in the Scrum team who is responsible for the smooth functioning of the team. Now, let's look at the responsibilities of a Scrum Master in detail. The below diagram (Fig. 5) depicts the key responsibilities of a Scrum Master.

Responsibilities of a Scrum Master

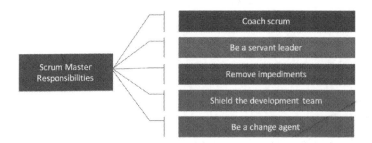

Fig. 5: Responsibilities of a Scrum Master

Coach Scrum

A Scrum Master teaches the values and principles of Scrum to the team. He observes how the team is using Scrum and helps them to being a mature Scrum team.

A Scrum Master ensures that the Scrum ceremonies are held each time and that the Product Owner and the Development Team work hand in hand with each other. He mentors the Development Team such that they are self-organizing and can assign the tasks to themselves. He insists on collaboration with each other.

Be a servant leader

A Scrum Master is often called a servant leader who serves the Product Owner, the Development Team and the organization. He ensures that there are no impediments to the progress of the team.

He coaches the agile best practices to the team and removes their impediments. He helps the team to achieve its goals and to perform at its highest level. A Scrum Master has great listening skills. He acts with empathy towards the team.

The difference between a traditional project manager and a Scrum Master is that a traditional project manager assigns work or tasks to the project team and seeks status from them on regular basis, whereas a Scrum Master mentors the team such that they can assign tasks to themselves and discuss their progress freely with each other.

Remove impediments

Impediments are any roadblocks or issues that block the team to deliver a valuable piece of software during a Sprint, or any problem that restricts the progress of the team. Impediments are problems that can't be solved by the Development Team on their own and are beyond the self-organization of the Development Team. In other words, any problem that affects the expected capacity of the team during a Sprint is called an impediment. A Scrum Master creates an environment of trust and encourages the Development Team to discuss impediments. A Scrum Master also analyzes the impediments to check if the problems are indeed impediments or if they are temporary blocks that can be resolved by the Development Team.

Some of the common impediments are listed as below:

a) Unplanned absence of a team member
b) Undesired changes in the team structure
c) Lack of technical skills
d) Unavailability of the Product Owner
e) An indecisive Product Owner
f) Conflict between the team members
g) External pressure from management

Another example of a common impediment is the non-availability of technical team members during scheduled Scrum ceremonies. If the team is not co-located and works from multiple locations across different time zones, it becomes difficult for some members to join the meetings.

A Scrum Master removes impediments, and keeps a track of the same. He, then, leverages the information during the Scrum ceremonies to improve the existing processes and minimize impediments.

A Scrum Master also ensures complete transparency to impediments. He may create a visual representation to track the status of impediments. Sometimes, a Scrum Master needs to take bold decisions to remove impediments for the team.

Shield the development team

A Scrum Master protects the Development Team from exterior interferences so that the team can focus on the committed work for the current iteration.

Often, there are external or management pressures on the Development Team that have the potential to impact the team's anticipated capacity during the Sprint. A manager may require the Development Team to attend a mandatory training, participate in an unplanned event, or fix an urgent production issue. These unplanned activities may impact the team's planned work during the Sprint. A Scrum Master shields the team from such adhoc activities.

Be a change agent

A Scrum Master acts as a change agent and mentors the leaders of an organization to adopt Scrum. He meets with other Scrum Masters in the organization to increase the adoption of Scrum in the organization.

A Scrum Master keeps a track of all the impediments or the problems that can't be solved by the team on their own. He, then, engages with other Scrum Masters and discusses any common or recurring impediments to the teams. A Scrum Master ensures that these impediments are visible to leaders of the organization such that organizational changes can be made to minimize the impediments and increase the effectiveness of the teams.

C. Development Team

Scrum Development Team is cross functional in nature which means that it is composed of all the different roles (designers, developers, testers etc.) required to deliver value at the end of each iteration.

In Waterfall or traditional project management, architects design the system interactions, developers build the code, and a separate team executes detailed functional and non-functional testing on the code to validate the code against the documented requirements. This usually leads to mismatch between what the architects have designed as compared to what was built, and finally what gets tested.

In Scrum, the Development Team performs all these functions – analyze, design, develop and test, within each iteration or cycle. The team works very closely together as one cohesive unit. This minimizes any gap between analyze, design, development, and testing of the product feature during the Sprint.

The Development Team is self-organizing and is typically five to nine people in size, such that it is small enough to remain agile and large enough to complete significant work within an iteration. The term 'self-organizing' team means that team is mature enough to assign tasks to themselves and resolve their day-today problems or roadblocks on their own.

The Development Team participates in Scrum ceremonies such as Backlog Grooming, Iteration Planning, Daily Stand up, Sprint Review, and Sprint Retrospective. We will discuss Scrum ceremonies in the next chapter.

The below diagram (Fig. 6) depicts the key responsibilities of a Scrum Development Team to participate in Iteration or Sprint Planning, contribute to Backlog Grooming, perform work during the Sprint or Iteration, inspect, and adapt to the feedback.

Responsibilities of the Development Team

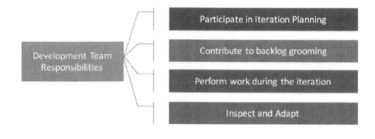

Fig. 6: Responsibilities of the Development Team

Participate in Iteration Planning:

A development team actively participates in the Iteration Planning or Sprint Planning meeting along with Scrum Master, Product Owner, and other stakeholders. The team sets aside the time required for different Scrum ceremonies during the Sprint, and actively participates in the meetings.

During a Sprint Planning meeting, the team asks enough questions to the Product Owner that they can convert the User Stories of the Product Backlog to detailed tasks. The team also commits to the User Stories that they can complete in the current iteration or Sprint. The team discusses any known issues or dependencies during the planning meeting and confirms the acceptance criteria for the committed work.

Contribute to Backlog Grooming

The development team participates in the Backlog Grooming meeting along with Product Owner and Scrum Master. During this meeting, the team assists the Product Owner to create and prioritize the User Stories in the backlog. The team asks questions to the Product Owner such that the items at the top of the backlog are groomed, refined, and ready. The team also provides a high-level estimation of the items that are at the top of the backlog.

Perform work during the iteration

The main responsibility of the Development Team is to analyze, design, build and test the work items or User Stories that have been committed for the current iteration or Sprint.

The team assign work to themselves, and start working on the detailed tasks in the Sprint Backlog. They track their actual hours against the assigned tasks every day. The team ensures that the completed work meets the Definition of

Done and the acceptance criteria defined by the Product Owner.

Inspect and Adapt

The Development Team participates in the progress inspection during the Sprint and then adapts accordingly.

The team participates in daily stand-up meetings to discuss their daily progress and impediments. They also participate in the Sprint Retrospective meeting at the end of each Sprint to discuss what worked well, and what needs to be improved for the next Sprint. The team continuously strives to increase their delivery and effectiveness.

It is very important that all the three Scrum roles – Product Owner, Scrum Master and Development Team work hand in hand with each other.

Summary

In this chapter, I described the three Scrum roles - Product Owner, Scrum Master, and the Development Team. A Product Owner decides what will be developed and in which order. A Scrum Master acts as a Scrum coach and mentors the team to adapt Scrum principles. A Development Team is a cross-functional and self-organizing team that executes the work. I also explained the key responsibilities for each Scrum role. In the next chapter, I will emphasize on the five Scrum ceremonies.

Chapter 4 – Scrum Ceremonies

In Scrum, work is performed in iterations or time boxed cycles (usually 2 weeks to one month). These iterations are called as Sprints. The work completed in each Sprint brings value to the customer. Sprints always have a fixed start and end date and should be of the same duration. A new Sprint starts immediately after the conclusion of the previous Sprint. It is not recommended to make scope or team changes in the middle of a Sprint. A Sprint can only be cancelled by the Product Owner when Sprint goal becomes obsolete.

There are five key Scrum ceremonies that must occur for each iteration or Sprint.

The five Scrum ceremonies are as below:
- Product Backlog Grooming
- Sprint Planning
- Daily Stand-Up
- Sprint Review
- Sprint Retrospective

Product Backlog Grooming

The Product Owner works closely with the Development Team to refine, prioritize and estimate the work list. This activity of creating, refining, estimating and prioritizing the work list is known as Product Backlog Grooming.

The best time to have Backlog Grooming is two to three business days prior to the start of the next Sprint. A Product Owner or a Scrum Master facilitates this meeting. During this meeting, the team focusses only on the stories that are likely to be started in the next Sprint. The team ensures that the items at the top of the backlog are detailed, estimated, and ready for the upcoming Sprint.

The Product Backlog Grooming meetings give an opportunity to the team to familiarize themselves with the upcoming work and discuss any known issues or dependencies related to the prioritized work. The regular grooming meetings ensure that the Sprint Planning meetings run smoothly.

Unlike Waterfall or traditional method where all the requirements are detailed and aligned upfront, Scrum expects the Product Backlog to be continually groomed during the iterations or Sprints. Unlike Waterfall, only the top items or prioritized User Stories are refined in the grooming meeting.

Sprint Planning

Sprint planning is an activity that takes place at the beginning of each Sprint. It is a collaborative effort between a Product Owner, a Scrum Master and the Development Team. The Scrum Master facilitates this meeting.

During Sprint Planning, the Product Owner and the Development Team agree on a Sprint goal for the upcoming Sprint. The Product Owner describes the highest priority items in the Product Backlog. The team aligns what User Stories are ready to start to meet the Sprint goal. The prioritized User Stories that are ready, then, become part of the Sprint Backlog. The Sprint Backlog is a list of User Stories that will be worked upon by the Development Team in the upcoming Sprint.

The Development Team asks questions and creates detailed tasks against the stories in the Sprint Backlog. The team also estimates their effort for the detailed tasks and commits to complete the stories in the Sprint Backlog within the upcoming Sprint.

This ceremony is usually a time-boxed activity spanning from 6-8 hours for a one month Sprint to 1-2 hours for a shorter Sprint.

Further details on how the team decides the User Stories that form a Sprint Backlog can be read in subsequent chapters.

Daily Stand-Up

Daily stand-up is a 15-minute activity that takes place each day of the Sprint, at the same time. Everyone stands during this event and each of the team member speaks to below three questions:

- What did I do yesterday?
- What will I do today?
- What are the impediments that prevent me to make progress?

Typically, these meetings are held in the same location and at the same time every day.

The intent of these meetings is not to provide a status update to the Scrum Master.

Each member of the team should address his or her comments to other team members and carefully listen to other members' updates.

The stand-up meeting is not meant for any technical discussion between the team. A Scrum Master should mentor the team and ensure that stand-up meetings stay short and relevant to the three questions.

Sometimes, when a new User Story gets created, or when senior management need urgent status updates, Scrum Master tends to discuss those items in the daily stand-up meeting. This practice should be discouraged. A Scrum Master may schedule a separate meeting with the team to address any new User Stories or urgent action items.

The daily Scrum is a daily planning activity that helps a self-organizing team to perform better.

Scrum has used the terms 'chickens' and 'pigs' to distinguish who should participate during the daily Scrum versus who should simply observe. There's a story in Scrum about a chicken and a pig. Both decide to open a restaurant. The pig asked the chicken what should they call the restaurant. The chicken replies: "Ham and Eggs!" The pig then replies:

"No thanks! I'd be committed. You'd only be involved." Most people consider the entire Scrum team as pigs, and anyone who is not on the Scrum team as a chicken. Originally, some people considered the Product Owner as a chicken, as he or she is not required to join the daily Scrum meetings.

Sprint Review

This is a scheduled inspect and adapt activity in which the stakeholders review the completed work at the end of each Sprint. The Scrum team, sponsors, stakeholders, customers and any other interested people attend this event.

In this ceremony, the Scrum team shows the work accomplished in the Sprint. The team provides a demo of the product with new features or work that was completed in the Sprint.

This ceremony provides an opportunity to the Scrum team to showcase their completed work, obtain feedback from the stakeholders, and gain visibility of their work. Prior to the Sprint review meeting, the Scrum team should align the structure of the demonstration and discuss the responsibilities of each member for the meeting. The preparation time for this meeting is usually limited to two hours.

It is a collaborative working session to inspect the work completed in the Sprint and to seek feedback on what should be done next. The meeting should not be used as an acceptance or sign-off meeting. Prior to this meeting, the Product Owner should have already reviewed the User Stories that were marked as 'Done'. Any incomplete User Stories that moved back to the Product Backlog should also be discussed during this meeting to ensure complete transparency of the remaining work.

The feedback received from the stakeholders during this meeting should be welcomed. Any requests to add or enhance the features of the product should be added to the Product Backlog for later refinement and prioritization.

Typically, this meeting lasts for around two hours for a two-week Sprint, or one hour for a one week Sprint.

Sprint Retrospective

This is second inspect and adapt activity at the end of each Sprint. This usually happens after the Sprint Review ceremony and before the next Sprint begins. During this meeting, the entire team comes together and discusses what worked best for the Sprint, what went wrong during the Sprint, and what can be done to improve the next Sprint. The purpose of this ceremony is to inspect and adapt the existing process in an open, honest, and constructive environment.

This meeting is facilitated by the Scrum Master. There are many ways to conduct a Sprint Retrospective meeting. One of the common ways is that the Scrum Master draws three columns on a whiteboard – first with a happy face, second with a sad face, and third column with a neutral face. The team members write their comments under each column and then discuss the improvements that can be made to the process. The Scrum Master documents and tracks the action items that result from this meeting. Another variation is the approach where the team members are asked what should the team start doing, stop doing, or continue doing. The team brainstorms and comes up with an initial list of ideas. Then, the team votes on specific items to focus on during the coming Sprint.

This ceremony builds the team's self-management and ownership. It gives the team an opportunity to make process improvements and improve their productivity for the next Sprint.

Summary

In this chapter, I explained the five Scrum ceremonies. Product Backlog Grooming ceremony helps to refine, prioritize, and estimate the Product Backlog. The Sprint Planning ceremony allows the team to decide the stories that will be worked upon in the upcoming Sprint. The team breaks down the User Stories into detailed tasks and provides an estimate to complete the tasks. The Daily Stand-Up ceremony requires each team member to answer three questions and highlight impediments to their work. The Sprint Review ceremony gives an opportunity to the stakeholders to review the completed work and provide their feedback at the end of each Sprint. The Sprint Retrospective ceremony focuses on process improvements to increase the efficiency and effectiveness of the team.

Chapter 5 – Scrum Artifacts

An artifact is a tangible by-product or item produced during the product development. In this chapter, we will familiarize ourselves with the Scrum artifacts.

The key Scrum artifacts are listed below (see Fig. 7):

- ✓ Product Backlog
- ✓ Sprint Backlog
- ✓ Potentially shippable product increment
- ✓ Process improvement feedback

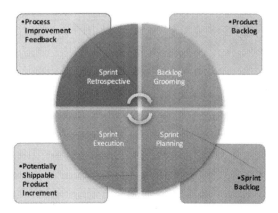

Fig. 7: Scrum artifacts

Product Backlog

A Product Backlog is a prioritized list of desired product features. It is comprised of backlog items that are nothing but the desired features or functionality for the product along with bugs, technical work and any research that needs to be done. The backlog items within the Product Backlog are sorted in the order of priority such that the highest priority item is at the top of the list.

The Product Owner is responsible for the content and priority of the items in the Product Backlog. The Scrum Master also assists the

Product Owner to maintain the Product Backlog.

Think about the earlier website development case study. The entrepreneur created a list of features for his website and listed them in the order of importance. Such a list of prioritized items is known as Product Backlog.

A sample Product Backlog for our website development effort will look like this:

- As an entrepreneur, I want to have a website that shows all my company's products and services.
- As an entrepreneur, I want my website to have an online payments capability for the customers.
- As an entrepreneur, I want the website to track the unique visitors.
- As an entrepreneur, I want to post my blogs on the website.
- As an entrepreneur, I want to market my products to the customers.
- As an entrepreneur, I want the website to display earned loyalty points for the customers.

o   As a site visitor, I want to see the benefits and pricing of all available products and services.
o   As a site visitor, I want to compare multiple products.
o   As a site visitor, I want to read FAQs.
o   As a customer, I want my payment transactions to be secure.
o   As a customer, I want to see multiple shipping options and rates on the site.
o   As a customer, I want to redeem my earned loyalty points on the website.
o   As a site admin, I can revise the pricing of any product or service.
o   As a site admin, I can add new products to the website.
o   As a site admin, I can delete any product or service from the website.
.....................and so on.

The Product Backlog items are usually written at a very high level and are called Epics. Sometimes, an Epic is also called as a large story. An Epic is usually broken down into smaller pieces known as User Stories. If you group related stories together, that collection of User Stories is known as a Theme. Let's look at

Fig. 8 to understand the difference between an Epic, Story and a Theme.

Fig. 8: Epic vs Story vs Theme

During the Product Backlog Grooming meeting, the prioritized items at the top of the Product Backlog are broken down into User Stories. The User Stories are then refined and estimated.

Sprint Backlog

The Sprint Backlog is an ordered list of Product Backlog items that the Development Team committed to complete during the current sprint. These items are taken from the top of the Product Backlog during the Sprint Planning meeting.

The Sprint Backlog comprises of detailed tasks associated with each User Story in the Sprint Backlog. The Sprint Backlog should contain all different types of tasks associated with a User Story e.g. learning new technology, co-ordination with dependent teams, creating detailed design, development, executing unit testing, executing browser compatibility tests, completing code reviews, enhancing the automated test suite, supporting continuous integration, deploying to test environment, etc. The team should refer to the 'Definition of Done' and ensure that all tasks required to create a working quality software are listed. The tasks in the Sprint Backlog are estimated in terms of hours.

Let's understand the difference between a Product Backlog and a Sprint Backlog with our earlier website development example. The first epic in our sample Product Backlog with the topmost priority was:

o   As an entrepreneur, I want to have a website that shows all my company's products and services.

When we break this one epic into multiple stories, the top User Stories of the sample Product Backlog look like below:

- As an entrepreneur, I want a list of all products to be displayed.
- As an entrepreneur, I want the image or icon of all products to be displayed on the home page.
- As an entrepreneur, I want to have a homepage that displays a short description along with the associated image for all products.
- As an entrepreneur, I want to display the detailed specifications for each of my products.
- As an entrepreneur, I want to display the benefits for each of my products.
- As an entrepreneur, I want to display the pricing of my latest products and services upfront on the homepage.

During a Sprint Planning meeting, the Product Owner and the team decide which stories can be taken up for the current Sprint. The stories that the team agrees to complete in the current Sprint then forms the Sprint Backlog.

Thus, if Team B decides to work on below two stories for the current Sprint, then this list becomes the Sprint Backlog for the team.

- o As an entrepreneur, I want a list of all products to be displayed.
- o As an entrepreneur, I want the image or icon of all products to be displayed on the home page.

Potentially Shippable Product Increment

The outcome of the work performed within a Sprint is known as Potentially Shippable Product Increment. The team builds a Potentially Shippable Product Increment at the end of every Sprint. During Sprint Review meeting, the team provides a demo of this product increment to the stakeholders.

Being potentially shippable does not mean that the results must be delivered to the customers at the end of each Sprint. It rather means that the work performed is of such a high quality that it can be delivered to the customer, if Product Owner desires.

In our website development example, at the end of the first Sprint, Team B provided a demo of the website to the entrepreneur. The website displayed a product list along with the associated image or icon of the product. Team B doesn't need to launch their website yet, however, the work completed is a potentially shippable product increment and has the potential to go live, if desired by the entrepreneur.

Potentially Shippable Product Increment or the work completed in a Sprint should meet the 'Definition of Done' which is a set of conditions that must be met before a User Story can be marked as 'Done'. This set of conditions is jointly defined by the Product Owner and the Development Team at the start of the release or the Sprint. It ensures that the work completed in the Sprint meets the required quality standards and is capable to be launched in a live environment, if requested.

Process Improvement Feedback

The feedback received from the team during the Sprint Retrospective meeting is known as Process Improvement Feedback. This feedback is targeted on the process itself, and is very valuable to make things better!

Scrum enables an organization to be engaged in continuous process improvement. The process feedback gathered during a Sprint Retrospective meeting encourages the team and the organization to improve their existing processes. A Scrum Master should learn how to facilitate a Sprint Retrospective meeting effectively, track the valuable feedback received, and encourage small incremental improvements to the existing process in the upcoming Sprint.

During one of my Sprint Retrospective meetings, the team expressed concerns that most of the stories are blocked due to dependency with another Scrum team. The other product team had a separate Product Owner and a separate Product Backlog. Their priorities were different than those of our team. I met with the Scrum Master of the other team, and facilitated discussions between the two Product Owners. Later, I invited the Product Owner, and the key members of the other Scrum team to our Sprint Review meetings. This process improvement helped to bridge the communication gap between the two teams and removed the team's impediment to work on the prioritized User Stories.

Summary

In this chapter, I described the artifacts of the Scrum framework. The Product Backlog is a prioritized list of work items owned by the Product Owner. The Sprint Backlog is the list of work items or User Stories that the team commits to complete in the upcoming Sprint. At the end of each Sprint, the team delivers a Potentially Shippable Product Increment that meets the Definition of Done. The feedback received from the Scrum team during a Sprint Retrospective ceremony is called the Process Improvement Feedback. The Scrum Master leverages this feedback to make incremental improvements to the existing processes. In the next chapter, I will emphasize on Agile Scrum principles.

Chapter 6 – Agile Principles

Scrum is one of the Agile development methodology and follows the principles mentioned in the Agile manifesto. The manifesto for Agile Software Development covers the four principles (Fig. 9):

o Individuals and interactions over processes and tools
o Working software over comprehensive documentation
o Customer collaboration over contract negotiation
o Responding to change over following a plan

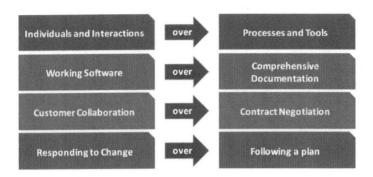

Fig. 9: Agile Manifesto

Principle 1: Individuals and interactions over processes and tools

The Agile Manifesto values people and their interactions over processes and tools. When organizations put processes and tools over people and interactions among them, they focus on conformity to processes and tools. Such organizations have clear defined processes and an extensive set of tools to implement the processes. However, this restricts new ideas and makes it hard for people to conform to processes. People start creating their own ways and excuses to work around the processes.

However, when people and interactions are put over the processes and tools, then it creates a people centric environment with high productivity, new ideas, mutual trust, and cooperation. An Agile environment encourages ideas and interactions over processes and tools. Some of the benefits of having a people focused environment are as below:

- High performing teams
- Motivated individuals
- Clear and effective communication
- Increased accountability
- Self-organizing teams
- Higher job satisfaction
- High productivity
- Increased collaboration
- Mutual trust and respect
- Innovation and growth

The below diagram (Fig. 10) represents this principle to focus on people and their interactions over processes and tools. The left-hand side represents a group of people who collaborate with each other and the right side represents the processes and tools deployed in an organization.

Fig. 10: Individuals and interactions over processes and tools

The traditional plan-driven and sequential processes such as Waterfall encourage conformance to a defined process. The objective of a plan driven approach is to follow a sequential set of steps to achieve same result every time. However, with Scrum, the goal is to encourage variability. In Scrum, the product being developed is complex and unique in nature. Here, we don't expect to achieve same results each time. Instead, the team's focus is to encourage new ideas, and develop a unique product. There is an increased need for collaboration, research, and experimentation.

Principle 2: Working software over comprehensive documentation

The Agile Manifesto values working software over comprehensive documentation. The focus for an Agile Software Development team should be to develop working software rather than creating detailed requirements and producing comprehensive documentation.

The traditional plan-driven sequential development assumes that upfront detailed planning and documentation will work best. The assumption is that we can get all the requirements and plans correct up front. The fact is that it is very unlikely to document all the requirements and create detailed plans correctly at the beginning of the project.

In Scrum, we acknowledge that we can't get all the requirements and plans right up front. Scrum is based on iterative and incremental development. Iterative development assumes that some rework and improvement is required to make things right. For example, a proof of concept may highlight the shortcomings of a technical design solution. The team then reworks on the technical solution to make it more efficient. Incremental development is building small portions of the product rather than building it all at once. The product is broken down into small features so that the team can build few prioritized features first, adapt based on their learning, and then build more features of the product.

With traditional project management, the team spends several months in creating detailed requirements, design documents, and plans at the start of the project, and by the time the project reaches the test phase, the requirements change, and now the team must modify the baselined requirements, design documents, and their plans to match to the new scope of work. This results in huge rework and waste.

With Scrum, the team focusses on a small prioritized set of features or requirements and plans to develop those first. The team continually adapts based on their experience. They demonstrate their completed work at the end of each iteration and thus, any missed requirements, new features, or comments find their way to the Product Backlog. With this adaptive approach, the wasteful effort is reduced to a minimum.

With traditional sequential development, the team spends a lot of their effort and resources in creating upfront artifacts that provide no direct customer value. Scrum, on the other hand, is customer value-centric development. It is an incremental approach where highest priority items are continuously built in each iteration, thereby delivering direct value to the customers.

I managed several projects both in Waterfall and Scrum methodology. I remember a Waterfall project which lasted almost two years. We spent almost five months in analyze phase, created extensive documentation for existing and new process flows, had several discussions to figure out each corner case scenario, and created a massive requirements document. Despite our huge effort during analyze phase, the team struggled during testing. The reasons being:

- We received several change requests that resulted in a massive change to our documentation and caused re-work.
- The subject matter experts who participated in analyze discussions were no longer available during the test phase.
- It was hard to recall the analyze discussions that happened a while back.

With Scrum, we only refine the items on the top of the Product Backlog rather than capturing detailed requirements for the entire product. Next, the team works only on the prioritized, refined, and estimated items to create potentially shippable working software component at the end of every iteration. Thus, the problems faced with the traditional Waterfall approach are mitigated with Scrum.

The below diagram (Fig.11) represents this core Agile principle to prefer working software over comprehensive documentation.

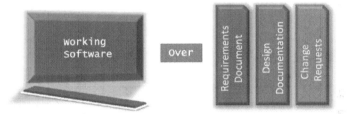

Fig. 11: Working software over comprehensive documentation

Scrum does not mean that we don't need to create any documentation. We should only create the minimal essential documentation that adds value to the work, and most importantly, we should create it only when we need it (also known as Just-In-Time manner).

Principle 3: Customer collaboration over contract negotiation

The Agile Manifesto values customer collaboration over contract negotiation. The Agile development team should have a close interaction with the customer, building a relationship of mutual trust, rather than having a binding up-front contract (or a written agreement) with the customer.

In a plan-driven sequential development, it is required that all important decisions are made upfront like requirements must be detailed and completed upfront, design must be reviewed and approved upfront, and so on. With Scrum, on the other hand, we believe that we have the least information at the start of the effort. We believe that we learn from our experiences, and thus, should not make important decisions until the last responsible moment (LRM). It is a strategy of not making a premature decision, delaying commitment, and keeping the options open until the cost of not making a decision becomes greater than the cost of making a decision.

With traditional or Waterfall approach, the primary focus is contract negotiation with the customer. The customer must approve the documented requirements based on his or her knowledge at the beginning of the project. Any changes, thereafter, are managed via a change control process or a re-negotiated contract, that does not give much flexibility to the customer. Also, the cost of change is more expensive late than it is early on. For example, a change made during design phase is less costly and requires less rework as compared to any change that is made during the test phase. Thus, to avoid late changes and high cost of change, the customer is under a tremendous pressure to ensure that all the requirements are accurately documented during the analyze phase. It is highly unlikely to accurately predict all the requirements at the beginning of the project which results in multiple change control requests during the project.

With Scrum, on the other hand, the primary focus is customer collaboration. The team works very closely with the customer and iteratively evolves the product features. If the Product Owner or any other stakeholder requires a change, a new User Story gets created on the

Product Backlog and is prioritized for the upcoming Sprint. The team collaborates with the Product Owner and embraces change.

The below diagram (Fig. 12) depicts the Agile principle that gives more importance to customer collaboration as compared to contract negotiation with the customer. In the below figure, the left-hand side represents a team of people who collaborate with each other and discuss new ideas, whereas, the right-hand side represents a contract with the customer.

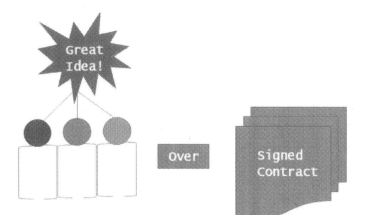

Fig. 12: Customer collaboration over contract negotiation

Principle 4: Responding to change over following a plan

The Agile Manifesto values responding to change over following a plan. The Agile team adapts a change easily as compared to a traditional project team.

With sequential project management, a detailed project plan is created that highlights the tasks under each project phase, interdependencies between the tasks, and resources assigned to each task. The project plan depicts the critical path of the project i.e. the tasks that are critical to be completed on-time as planned, or otherwise, will lead to a delay in the overall project schedule. The team heavily relies on this detailed project plan. Conformance to the plan is expected. Moreover, the cost of change rises rapidly over time. Late requirement changes result into huge rework, re-planning, and increased cost.

Scrum, on the other hand, does not conform to an upfront plan and embraces change. The cost of late change is much less in Scrum as compared to traditional plan based development. With Scrum, the artifacts are produced in Just-In-Time (JIT) fashion. For example, only the prioritized backlog items that will be worked upon in the next two Sprints are groomed. Similarly, the Scrum team documents the test scenarios only for the User Stories that are in-scope for the current Sprint. Thus, any change to the accepted User Stories only affect the artifacts related to that feature. The rework is minimal, keeping the cost of change low.

With iterative and incremental development approach, the Scrum team can quickly respond to a change and deliver a valuable product.

The below diagram (Fig. 13) depicts the Agile principle of responding to change over following a plan.

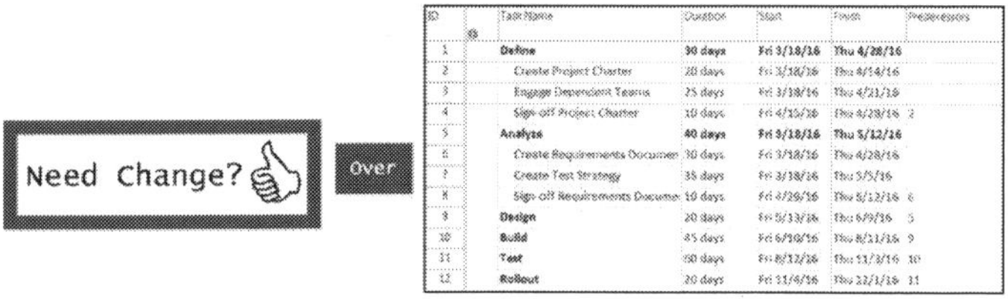

Fig. 13: Responding to change over following a plan

With traditional upfront planning approach, we make many assumptions that represent a significant risk to the project deliverables. However, with Scrum, we experiment different options, embrace change, and validate our assumptions fast. This reduces the overall risk on the product delivery.

Comparison

The below table provides a quick comparison of the plan-driven and the Scrum approach.

Plan-Driven Approach	Scrum Approach
Encourages conformance to processes and tools	Encourages people interactions
Comprehensive Documentation	Working Software
Restricts new ideas	Encourages experimentation and new ideas
Process centric environment	People centric environment
Contract negotiation	Customer collaboration
Conform to a plan	Embrace change
Requires continuous effort to motivate the team members	High performing, self-organizing, and motivated team
Low productivity	High productivity
Late changes require huge rework	Late changes are easily adopted with minimal

	rework
High cost of change	Low cost of change
Detailed project plan	Just-In-Time planning
Large possibility of a mismatch between requirements and the final product	Reduced mismatch between requirements and the final product
Likely to have unhappy customers	Likely to have delighted customers
Late customer feedback	Fast and frequent customer feedback
Requires upfront decisions	Decisions wait till the last responsible moment (LRM)
Low interaction with business sponsors	High collaboration with Product Owner

Fig. 14: Comparison between Scrum and traditional plan-driven approach

Summary
In this chapter, I described the core Agile principles that are the foundation for the Scrum framework. I also compared these principles with those of the plan-driven traditional

development approach. The purpose of this comparison was to enable you to evaluate and adapt the approach that is well suited for your organization and/or effort. In the next chapter, I will emphasize the importance of time-boxed iterations or Sprints.

Chapter 7 – Sprints

In Scrum, work is organized in iterations or cycles of one week to one month called Sprints. They are time boxed, short, have a consistent duration, have a goal, and produce a potentially shippable product increment that meets the team's Definition of Done.

Benefits of Time Boxing

Sprints have a specific start and end dates. During a Sprint, the team is expected to work at a sustainable pace to meet the Sprint goal. Inside this time box, the team works only on the prioritized User Stories that form the Sprint Backlog for the current Sprint.

The specific start and end dates create an urgency for the team to complete the work on time. The team must complete the work at the end of a Sprint and demonstrate their progress to product stakeholders. The inspect and adapt activity at the end of each Sprint allows the stakeholders to review the progress and align on the remaining work.

Benefits of Short Duration Sprints

Sprint are usually cycles of short duration. The short duration enables the team to generate fast feedback from the product stakeholders. With traditional plan-based development, the team receives customer feedback a long time after design and development. Requested changes result in huge rework and have a high cost of change. With Scrum, the customer feedback is received at the end of every Sprint which enables the team to adapt quickly.

The short duration allows the team to experiment different options, validate their assumptions early on, and uncover any risks. Short duration Sprints also limit the error or waste to the duration of a Sprint. If the team works on wrong items, the amount of time and the effort lost is limited by the duration of the Sprint.

Short duration Sprints help to keep the team's excitement high since team makes visible progress in a short duration. This keeps the team motivated and interested in the work. With traditional plan-driven development, the team delivers their work only at the end of the project. The long duration of the project makes it difficult for the team to stay focused and interested in the effort. Scrum, on the other hand, enables the team to deliver value at the end of every Sprint which gives them a feeling of being accomplished throughout the effort.

Benefits of Consistent Duration

As a rule, all Sprints should be of consistent duration. If a team agrees to have two-week Sprints, then all Sprints for that team must be of the same two-week duration. If there's a holiday during a Sprint, the overall available capacity of the team reduces, but the Sprint length does not get adjusted.

Consistent duration Sprints provide us a cadence which is nothing but a regular, predictable rhythm to Scrum effort. The regular cadence creates a familiarity to the timing of different Scrum ceremonies. It enables the team to focus on important value-added work, and predict the timing for repeated but necessary activities. With regular cadence, Scrum ceremonies can be scheduled in advance for many Sprints, and recurring invites can be sent to block everyone's calendar. This reduces the unnecessary overhead in scheduling Scrum ceremonies and ensuring availability of the participants.

Having a consistent duration also enables the team to forecast the amount of work or User Stories that it can complete in a Sprint. Since the duration of all Sprints is the same, the calculation of team's velocity becomes simple. Velocity is the amount of work a team can accomplish within a Sprint.

Sprint Goal

Each Sprint has a defined goal that describes the business value to be delivered in the Sprint. The rule is that the Sprint goal cannot be changed once the Sprint has started. The Product Owner commits to this rule and ensures that the Sprint goal is not altered during the Sprint. The Development Team commits to complete the User Stories in the

Sprint Backlog and meet the defined Sprint goal by the end of the Sprint. It is important that both the Product Owner and the Development team trust each other to meet their commitments.

The reason of not altering the Sprint goal after the start of the Sprint is to avoid the wastage of the effort already spent with Product Backlog grooming and Sprint Planning ceremonies. If the team started working on the User Stories, then that effort is also wasted with the change in the Sprint goal. Moreover, the mutual trust between the Product Owner and the Development Team will deteriorate.

However, if in some rare scenarios such as external market fluctuation, high severity production incident, or competitor announcement, it is found that the loss to continue the Sprint is more than the loss to change the Sprint goal, then Product Owner may decide to alter the Sprint goal in the middle of the Sprint. In such scenarios, the Product Owner should be completely transparent with the Development Team so that the team understands the need of the change and mutual trust is upheld.

In cases when the Sprint goal becomes completely invalid, the Scrum team aligns that the current Sprint does not add any value at all. In such cases, the Product Owner can abnormally terminate a Sprint. The abnormal termination of a Sprint is rare and happens when external circumstances or events have invalidated the Sprint goal. It negatively impacts the motivation of the team.

In such scenarios when the Product Owner terminates the current Sprint, the Scrum team performs a Sprint retrospective. The Scrum Master gathers the data from the retrospective, and works with the leadership to improvise existing processes and to minimize such events. The Product Owner works very closely with the Scrum team and re-prioritizes the Product Backlog. The Scrum team, then, starts planning for the next Sprint.

Definition of Done

The outcome of a Sprint is a potentially shippable product increment. As we learnt earlier, potentially shippable does not mean that the product should be shipped or launched in Production at the end of a Sprint. Rather, it means that the product should be of such a high quality that it could be shipped, if decided by the Product Owner.

For the product to be potentially shippable, it must meet the well-defined and aligned Definition of Done. It is a checklist of items that the team must complete before they can mark the work as 'Done' or 'Potentially Shippable'. A sample Definition of Done will look as below:

Sample Definition of Done
- Design Review Completed
- Code Completed
- Code Review Completed
- Unit Test Cases Written
- 100% Code Coverage Achieved
- Regression Test Library Updated
- Unit Testing Completed
- Functional Testing Completed
- Integration Testing Completed
- Regression Testing Completed
- Cross-Browser Compatibility Tested
- Device Testing Completed
- Performance Testing Completed
- Security Vulnerability Tested
- Defects Fixed and Closed
- Acceptance Testing Completed

The Definition of Done depends on several factors such as technology used, tools adopted by the organization, mandatory checks, nature of the work being developed, organization goals, test environments, etc. For example, if the product being developed is a responsive web application, then device testing and cross browser compatibility testing requirements must be met to ensure quality. Again, if an organization or a portfolio goal is to increase the code coverage of their applications, then any code being written must meet the code coverage related requirements before it can be shipped.

If a new product is being developed, the organization typically requires security vulnerability testing to be completed to ensure that the application has proper measures in place to avoid cross-site scripting attacks, SQL injection, command injection, insecure redirects, parameter tampering, insecure session management, unsafe password management, data catching, etc. In such cases, security vulnerability testing becomes part of the aligned Definition of Done to build secure applications.

Consider a product that has an automated regression test suite which enables the team to execute automated regression testing. If new features are being added to such a product, the task to update the regression test suite library becomes part of team's aligned Definition of Done such that the regression test suite library stays current during the development.

One of the most common task on the Definition of Done is to close all the open defects found during testing. However, if one of the defect can't be closed by the end of the Sprint, we must move the incomplete User Story back to the Product Backlog, and then re-prioritize the same to be completed in future Sprints. We don't extend the duration of a Sprint to close an open defect.

Often, organizational impediments don't allow us to have a perfect Definition of Done each Sprint. In one of the efforts that I worked on, the team could not execute the security vulnerability testing each Sprint. The reason being that a stable test environment was not available at the end of each Sprint. Thus, the team aligned to have a separate Sprint dedicated to security testing prior to their scheduled release. In this scenario, the team was not able to deliver a potentially shippable component each Sprint, as the code developed at the end of each Sprint was not ready to be launched in Production without the required security testing. Moreover, any defects from the security testing led to code fixes and rework. After few discussions with the release management team and senior leadership, it was aligned that a dedicated test environment will be set-up for the product team so that the security vulnerability testing is executed each Sprint. Thus, the team evolved its Definition of Done to deliver 'potentially shippable' components each Sprint.

Summary

In this chapter, I focused on describing the importance of Sprints in the Scrum framework. Sprints are short, time boxed, and consistent in duration. They have a goal which should not be altered unless the financial loss to continue the Sprint is more than the financial loss to change the goal or terminate a Sprint. Sprints should produce a potentially shippable component that meets the aligned Definition of Done. In the next chapter, I will describe User Stories.

Chapter 8 – User Stories

What are User Stories?

A User Story is a smallest piece of business value that a Scrum team can deliver in an iteration or a Sprint. They are written in a simple format that makes them understandable to both business and technical team. They are easy to be refined progressively.

With plan-driven traditional development, the requirements are written and detailed upfront. However, the fact is that you can't create a complete exhaustive list of requirements upfront as new requirements reveal themselves during the design and development of the product. With Scrum, we don't write all the requirements upfront.

Instead, we create placeholders for the requirements, called Product Backlog Items (PBIs). Initially the PBIs are large, and there is very little detail associated with them. The prioritized PBIs are then refined and detailed during the Product Backlog Grooming meeting. The PBIs are usually written in the form of User Stories. They represent the desired features of a product and are usually written in a conversational style.

A User Story is typically written in a format that represents the user role, the goal (what the user role wants to achieve), and the benefit (the reason to achieve the goal). The format is: As a <user role>, I want to <goal> so that <benefit>. Many people write User Stories on index cards or sticky notes. The User Stories act as placeholders for the desired features of the product and need not capture all the details upfront. As and when the User Stories are refined, the additional details are captured.

There are multiple levels of User Stories with different amount of details associated with them. The highest level or User Stories that have the least amount of detail in them are called Epics. Epics are written at a very high level and represent the work that can span an entire release or multiple releases. Epics reside in the Product Backlog, and are never part of the Sprint Backlog. They represent a bucket or a collection of User Stories and act as a starting point to help create detailed User Stories in future. The next level of User Stories that represent a large effort and span multiple Sprints are called large Product Backlog Items (PBIs) or sometimes referred to as Features. They too reside in the Product Backlog, and don't fit into a single Sprint. The lowest level of User Stories that have the maximum amount of details associated with them are typically called User Stories or sometimes called as Sprintable Stories. These represent small effort that can be completed within a single Sprint. They reside in both Product Backlog and Sprint Backlog. A group of related User Stories is termed as a Theme. Themes are the bundles of stories that have something in common.

Each User Story has an acceptance criteria or a list of conditions that must be met before the story can be accepted by the Product Owner. The acceptance conditions are an important way for the Product Owner to validate if the story has been developed correctly. These are primarily written to assist the Product Owner to review and accept the work. These are not the only conditions that the team must meet. As we learnt earlier, the team also ensures that the User Story meets the aligned Definition of Done such that the product increment is potentially shippable at the end of the Sprint.

Writing Good User Stories

It is important to write good stories. A well written User Story must meet the criteria of Bill Wake's INVEST acronym:

I – Independent: User Stories should be written in such a way that they are independent or at least loosely coupled with one another. The stories that are dependent on other stories introduce a lot of complexity in estimation and prioritization. For example, a User Story that is dependent on three other User Stories can't be estimated until the other three User Stories are estimated. The prioritization of such User Stories also become difficult. It is best to write stories in such a way that interdependencies between the stories is minimized.

N – Negotiable: User Stories should be written in such a way that they are negotiable. This means that stories should leave some room for the stakeholders to discuss and negotiate the details. The conversation allows the details to be refined by the team. It also ensures that the team develops a good understanding of the desired functionality. With plan-driven sequential development, the upfront requirements document must capture all the details and possible variations. This approach does not allow any negotiation once the requirements document is approved. Thus, the development team works on their assumptions and often, the final product does not meet the initial requirements. Such problems are minimized with Scrum.

V – Valuable: User Stories must be written in such a way that they are valuable to the Product Owner. In other words, User Stories should deliver value to a customer or an end user of the product. Sometimes, there are technical stories that are valuable to the development team but do not deliver any direct value to the Product Owner. In such cases, it is important that the Product Owner understands the value that the technical story will ultimately deliver and the reasons why he should prioritize and pay for the same. Ideally, we should not have technical stories in the Product Backlog. The technical stories should either be written as tasks associated with a business valuable story or baked into the aligned Definition of Done. Thus, all User Stories should be written such that they are valuable to the Product Owner.

E – Estimatable: User Stories should be estimatable by the development team. An estimate is an indicative measure of the size of the story. It indicates how much effort, cost and time will be needed to develop the story. The User Stories should be written in such a way that they are easy to estimate. If the team is not able to estimate the size of a User Story, then the story is either too big or too ambiguous. In such cases, the Product Owner works closely with the Development Team to break down the story into smaller stories and to refine the story. A well written User Story should be estimatable.

S – Small: User Stories should be written in such a way that they are small enough to be completed within few hours or days. If we have a two-week Sprint, we don't want to have a two-week size story, because the risk to not finishing the story by the end of the Sprint is too high. As we learnt earlier, we have User Stories with different degree of details associated with them such as Epic, Feature, and Sprintable Stories. In Scrum, we don't break down all Epics and Features into small Sprintable Stories up front. We only break down the top priority Epics and Features such that the team has small stories available for the next two Sprints.

T – Testable: User Stories should be written in a way that they are testable. Being testable means that they should have a strong acceptance criteria associated with them. The acceptance conditions help the Product Owner to review and accept the work. They also help the Development Team to correctly estimate the size of the story and develop the work as mutually aligned.

Not all stories will have an acceptance criteria defined. Epics and Features are too big and don't need to be testable. Once they are broken down into Sprintable Stories, they need to have an acceptance criteria associated with them. Some people write non-functional stories into the Product Backlog and then struggle to define an acceptance criteria for such stories.

For example, the User Story to have the system availability as 99.99% is a non-functional story and does not provide any direct value to the Product Owner. It is best not to write such stories into the Product Backlog. Instead, any technical and non-functional requirements should be listed into the aligned Definition of Done such that the team can deliver a potentially shippable product increment at the end of each Sprint.

Discovery of User Stories

How do Product Owners write User Stories? There are several ways to gather the needs of customers. Typically, the Product Owners hold several discussions with other stakeholders and come up with a product strategy and few large User Stories or Epics. A better approach is to conduct a discovery workshop to start with. This workshop promotes high level of participation from the stakeholders, helps to align the product goals, and discover large User Stories or Epics to meet the product goal. The workshop typically includes the Product Owner, Scrum Master, Development Team, the sponsor, end users, dependent teams, and other stakeholders. The format, the agenda, the participants, and the timing of this planning workshop differs for each organization.

In general, the discovery workshop starts when the sponsor or the Product Owner shares the product vision with the working group. The working group then writes their ideas about the product goals on sticky notes. The facilitator collects the sticky notes and groups them under categories or headings. These categories or headings are nothing, but large User Stories or Epics which act as a placeholder for writing detailed User Stories in future.

The next exercise, which I personally like, is reviewing the user roles or personas. It is very interesting to understand the product's primary and secondary audiences or users, their behavior patterns, their goals, their pain points, and their limitations. This exercise provides a lot of insight to the working group and helps them to think from the user's perspective.

The working group then begins to brainstorm on the desired features of the product to meet the identified product goals. In this exercise, the group typically dumps their ideas onto a whiteboard and then votes for the top five features desired for the product. Dot voting is a popular technique to facilitate voting in such scenarios. In this technique, each participant will come to the whiteboard and draw a dot against the feature that has his or her vote. The items that have the maximum number of dots are accepted as the top priorities. These top priority features are then written as stories and represent a bundle of Sprintable User Stories.

Another interesting activity is when the working group divides into teams, focuses on the primary persona and top features, and builds scenarios or use cases for those features. This exercise helps the working group to dig deeper into the top features from the user's perspective. The Product Owner leverages the output of this exercise to create more stories into the Product Backlog.

The fact is that there is no standard way to generate User Stories. Some organizations prefer top-down approach while others prefer bottom-up approach. The top-down approach is to define the large User Stories or Epics first, and then drilling them down to Sprintable User Stories. The bottom-up approach, on the other hand, focuses on creating Sprintable User Stories right from the start.

Sample User Stories

- As a student, I want this book to be available in eBook format so that I can read it on my laptop or phone.
- As an entrepreneur, I want to have a professional website so that I can sell my products and services.
- As a customer, I want to make online payments on the website so that I can save time.
- As a cardmember, I want to set recurring payments on the website so I can avoid the late payment fees.
- As a cardmember, I want to view my transactions on the website so that I can track my expenses.
- As a cardmember, I want to receive online statements so I can save paper.
- As a cardmember, I want to categorize my transactions so I can track the spend.
- As a cardmember, I want to view my prior statements on the website so I can track the spend across multiple years.
- As a cardmember, I want to view my card benefits on the website so I can understand what benefits I have.

- As a cardmember, I want to view my loyalty points on the website so I can redeem them when I desire.
- As a teacher, I want this book to be available to students in my class so that they can learn about Scrum.

Summary

In this chapter, I focused on User Stories, their standard format, and their different levels. I explained the differences between an Epic, a Feature, a Sprintable Story, and a Theme. I also described the techniques to write good User Stories. Then, I explained different strategies to gather User Stories. Lastly, I listed some sample User Stories for your easy reference. In the next chapter, we will discuss Technical Debt.

Chapter 9 – Technical Debt

In this chapter, we will learn about the term 'Technical Debt', its origin, main causes, and consequences. We will also learn how to manage technical debt.

Origin

Ward Cunningham introduced the concept of technical debt in 1992. He defined it as follows:

"Shipping first time code is like going into debt. A little debt speeds development so long as it is paid back promptly with a rewrite.... The danger occurs when the debt is not repaid. Every minute spent on not-quite-right code counts as interest on that debt. Entire

engineering organizations can be brought to a stand-still under the debt-load of an unconsolidated implementation, object oriented or otherwise."

Cunningham used the 'Technical Debt' metaphor to emphasize the benefits and limitations of speedy development. The metaphor was well received by both business and technical people as it resonates with financial debt. Like financial debt, technical debt accumulates interest with late repayment.

In 2004, Joshua Kerievsky describes 'design debt' in his article 'Refactoring to Patterns" and the associated costs. Then again in 2014, Grady Booch compared evolving cities to evolving software and described how lack of refactoring can lead to technical debt. He stated:

"The concept of technical debt is central to understanding the forces that weigh upon systems, for it often explains where, how, and why a system is stressed. In cities, repairs on infrastructure are often delayed and incremental changes are made rather than bold ones. So, it is again in software-intensive systems. Users suffer the consequences of capricious complexity, delayed improvements, and insufficient incremental change; the developers who evolve such systems suffer the slings and arrows of never being able to write

quality code because they are always trying to catch up."

Main causes of Technical Debt

Outdated design: Technical design that does not satisfy the Point-of-Arrival architecture. It means that if an application is built with an outdated or Point-of-Departure architecture which does not align with organizational blueprint, then the application will accumulate technical debt. Though such an application may have a quick time to market, it will require a rewrite of the code in future to meet the latest architecture standards. The more time the application takes to adapt to the latest architecture, the more effort will be required later for the rewrite. The more time the application will be available to the customers, the more difficult it will become to migrate the application and the customers to the new code.

Low code coverage: Code coverage is a measure used to describe the amount of code that gets executed during testing. The product with higher code coverage has less risk of uncovering unknown defects as compared to the application with low code coverage. If during Sprint Execution, the team does not spend time to improve the code coverage, and if the product is implemented with low code coverage, then there is an increased risk of experiencing undetected problems that may lead to poor customer satisfaction and brand damage. Moreover, when more features are added to the product, it is more difficult and time-consuming to rewrite the code and increase code coverage.

Lack of automated regression test suite: Regression testing is a type of testing that ensures that new features or enhancements to the product, or any new interfacing product does not impact the earlier working piece of software or product. These tests include validation of all past functionality that may be affected with the new changes. There are two ways to perform regression testing – manual and automated. In most cases, automated testing is more beneficial than manual testing to conduct regression testing. The reason being that the manual regression testing is very tedious and time-consuming. Moreover, each time there is a need to perform regression testing, any time you make changes to the code – add new features, enhance existing features, or make configuration changes, you will need to spend a large amount of time and effort with manual testing. Test automation makes the regression testing process very efficient. The test scripts can be automated once, and the automated test suite can be reused each time a change is introduced in the system. The test automation also ensures consistent results, reducing the possibility of human error. Though it takes time to automate the test scripts to start with, the benefits of having automated test suites overweigh the time and effort that is originally spent to create them.

Lack of regression test suites accumulate technical debt for the team. If new features are built without spending any time to create the regression test suite or to update the existing regression test suite, then it becomes more time consuming to automate the test scripts in future. The more you wait to create or update the regression test suite, the more features exist without automated tests, and the more time it takes to regression test the product.

Lack of Continuous Integration practice: Continuous Integration (CI) is a development practice that requires developers to integrate their code into the shared repository several times a day. With each new code integration, an automated build runs on the repository to detect early problems. The development teams can customize the frequency of this automated build to suit their needs. The automated build may trigger with each code integration or is scheduled to run at pre-determined times during the day. Continuous integration allows the development teams to catch issues early, reduce debugging time, minimize integration problems, and deliver software faster. If a product team does not integrate their code regularly with the shared repository, they will need to spend more effort during a later integration to isolate and fix the issues. The more the delay to integrate the code, the more technical debt the team accumulates.

Lack of appropriate testing: Testing plays an important role in delivering a quality software. There are different types of testing needs such as Unit Testing, Functional Testing, Integration Testing, Regression Testing, Stress Testing, Browser Compatibility Testing, Accessibility Testing, Responsive Web Design Testing, Performance Testing, Security Vulnerability Testing, User Acceptance Testing, and more. If you are creating a new web application and fail to execute Browser Compatibility Testing, then it is likely that the web application does not work properly with all the supported browsers. Similarly, if you are developing a responsive product, and you don't have enough devices or tools to execute the Responsive Web Design testing, then it is likely that the product will not display correctly on different devices. Often, teams don't have the required test data, testing tools, expertise, devices, test environment, funding, or time to execute the required tests. Any required testing that a development team delays or misses to execute will accumulate technical debt and will require more effort and resources to fix the defects later. It is much quicker and cheaper to fix defects at an early stage than to fix later.

Tightly coupled code: When the code components are highly dependent on each other, they are said to be tightly coupled. Such a code is not reusable and is difficult to maintain. If a product is built with tightly coupled code, any enhancements or even a minor change will have a huge impact to the code. The developers who build tightly coupled components create a technical debt for the organization.

Delayed refactoring: Refactoring is the code clean-up or the rewrite of the code. With new technology and evolving requirements, it becomes necessary to refactor the code to support latest technology and future requirements. If code refactoring is delayed, the features added on top of the existing code to support existing customers increase the technical debt. This technical debt must be paid when code refactoring is finally done.

Aggressive deadlines: Often, business or sponsors of a product require development effort to be completed before a deadline. The initial estimates and the projected velocity for the prioritized Product Backlog items are shared with the stakeholders. However, when the team starts working, more User Stories get added to the Product Backlog, more learning needs are identified, and more extensive research is required than anticipated. Thus, the actual velocity becomes slower than the projected velocity. This creates a lot of pressure on the developers to accelerate their velocity and meet the deadline. In such scenarios, the developers tend to take on technical debt to meet the aggressive dates.

There are many more causes for technical debt, including but not limited to, poorly written code, lack of alignment to industry standards, unreadable code, lack of code reviews, lack of appropriate documentation etc.

Consequences of Technical Debt
The more the technical debt, the more the severity of the consequences. Let's discuss few consequences with high technical debt.

Increased time to delivery: If a team takes on technical debt today, they increase the time required to deliver future work. It will take longer to deliver new features, enhancements, or fixes to customers in future. Though it may appear that skipping required testing, not creating regression test suite, or following an outdated design will speed up the current delivery, however, the fact is that the technical debt does not work in our best interests.

High number of defects: High technical debt results in significant number of defects in a product. Causes such as lack of testing, low code coverage etc. accumulate defects in a product which can lead to critical product failures, unexpected downtime, customer impact, potential brand damage, business loss, and more. Moreover, developers need to spend a lot of effort to fix these defects which takes their focus away from delivering new features.

Increased costs: As technical debt increases, costs to develop and maintain a product also increase. Causes such as lack of regression test suite, lack of continuous integration practice, developing tightly coupled code, delayed refactoring etc. lead to increased time and cost to deliver new features and to support the product. With increased costs, it becomes more and more difficult for the product to adapt to latest trends.

Low performance: As technical debt increases and it becomes more and more difficult to deliver new features, enhancements, or fixes to a product, the product starts to have a low performance. Increased page load time, unexpected issues, and unscheduled outages become common with low performance products. This negatively impacts the business of an organization.

Customer dis-satisfaction: High technical debt eventually leads to customer frustration and dis-satisfaction. A product with high technical debt has unresolved defects and low performance which leads to customer dis-satisfaction. Unsatisfied customers soon switch to another competitor product which results in loss of revenue for the organization.

Managing Technical Debt

An organization should enforce good technical practices to all the developers, including but not limited to technical design review, code review, automated regression suite, high code coverage, adequate testing, and continuous integration. This will limit the accrual of technical debt. The products that have accumulated technical debt should focus on refactoring to reduce technical debt and improve maintainability. I will now describe few techniques to manage technical debt for a product.

Have a strong Definition of Done: Having a strong Definition of Done minimizes the accrual of technical debt. The recommended technical practices must be listed in the Definition of Done. For example, tasks such as design review, code review, updating regression test suite, increasing code coverage, executing accessibility testing, browser compatibility testing, security vulnerability testing, or any other required testing must be completed prior to delivering a work item or a potentially shippable product increment.

Create visibility: Often, we don't make technical debt visible to our business partners, dependent teams, and other stakeholders. If technical debt is visible to a product sponsor, he or she will be able to understand the associated risks and allocate funding to minimize the same. For example, if a product has accumulated a high technical debt such that refactoring is the only option to reduce the debt, and if the sponsor is aware of the implications of this technical debt, then the product sponsor will fund the effort required to refactor the product in addition to the effort required to add new features to the product.

The tasks that can reduce the technical debt such as increasing code coverage, creating an automated test suite etc. should be added to the Product Backlog, and should be prioritized like other backlog items. This will ensure good visibility of the technical debt. However, some teams may like to create a Kanban board or a separate list to track the technical debt.

Prioritize Technical Debt: It is important to prioritize technical debt like product features. When there is a huge amount of technical debt, it is recommended that the team works on the highest priority task first. For example, if refactoring is the highest priority task required to reduce the technical debt, then developers should spend some time to refactor the code in each Sprint. The effort spent on reducing technical debt within a Sprint should be visible to the Product Owner and other stakeholders.

Incremental approach: Like product features, technical debt should also be built incrementally. Many teams tend to dedicate their entire Sprint for reducing technical debt. This approach is not recommended as it does not leave any room for value-added work to be delivered. However, if risks to continue the value-added work are significant, then the teams may plan to have a dedicated Sprint to reduce technical debt.

Summary

In this chapter, I explained the origin of technical debt. I also described the various causes that lead to technical debt. Then, I highlighted the consequences of technical debt. In the end, I described some of the ways to manage technical debt.

Chapter 10 – Estimation & Velocity

In this chapter, I will explain the need of estimation. Then, I will focus on estimation units and techniques. Later, I will describe the concept of Velocity and how it is used.

Why estimate?

The product sponsor who funds the development work wants to know the cost required to launch the product. The cost depends on how long will it take to deliver the product. Sometimes, the core product features required in a product are fixed or nonnegotiable, and the sponsor needs to know the duration and the cost required for the overall effort. Sometimes, you have a fixed release date, and the sponsor wants to know how many product features can be delivered within that duration. Or, you may have a fixed cost situation where you need to plan the features that you can deliver within the approved budget, and the duration for which you can sustain the team. Whatever maybe the situation, you will be required to estimate either the duration, cost, or scope for planning purposes. Thus, it is very important to estimate the size of the work items and measure the velocity or the rate at which we can get the work done. For example, if you must deliver the work worth 100 units, and you know that your team can complete 5 units in a two-week Sprint, then you know that your team will need about 20 Sprints or a total of 40 weeks to complete the required work. Again, if you must deliver a product within 20 weeks, and the team's average velocity is 5 units per two-week Sprint, then you know that the team can deliver about 50 units of work within that duration.

Estimation Units

Different units of estimation are used based on what we need to estimate and at what level. There are primarily two levels at which estimation is required - Product Backlog and Spring Backlog.

Most organizations estimate their Product Backlog Items (PBIs) in terms of Story Points. A Story Point is a relative estimation unit or a relative measure of complexity and size. It is believed that people are more comfortable and more accurate in providing relative estimates as compared to providing absolute estimates. For example, it may be difficult to estimate the actual length of the park, whereas it is much easier to compare the sizes of the two parks.

Story Points measure the size of the Product Backlog Item (PBI) relative to the size of another PBI. For example, if the PBI to display credit card transactions is estimated as 2 Story Points, and the PBI item to categorize the transactions by merchant is estimated as 4 Story Points, then it implies that the categorization story will take twice the effort as compared to the display transaction story. Let's take another example of two User Stories in the Product Backlog. The first User Story is to login into a website, while the second User Story is to display past records or transaction history for the user. It could be difficult to provide absolute estimates for these two User Stories, however, if you know that the first User Story to login into the website is worth 1 Story Point, then you can comfortably provide a relative estimate for the second User Story.

Most organizations estimate their Sprint Backlog Items in terms of the effort or hours required to complete the task. The tasks in the Sprint Backlog are detailed in nature which makes it easier for the team to provide an absolute estimate for them. For example, if a task is to replace an icon/image with a new one, then a developer can easily estimate the hours required to complete this task.

Estimation Techniques

For estimating Product Backlog Items (PBIs), the common technique that is used is called Planning Poker. This technique was first described by James Grenning and then by Mike Cohn. It is a consensus-based technique for relative estimation.

In this technique, the entire Scrum team participates. Each Development Team member is provided with a set of Planning Poker cards. On one side of a card, there is a number written in a Fibonacci sequence (0, 1, 2, 3, 5, 8, 13, 21, 34, 55 and so on). This sequence was first proposed by Mike Cohn, and is an appropriate scale to group similar size stories together and to separate out different size stories.

At first, the Product Owner describes the Product Backlog Item (PBI) to be estimated, and the team asks questions to clarify any assumptions and risks related to the specific PBI. Then, each developer privately selects a card that represent his or her Story Point estimate. On the count of three, everyone reveals the number on their card to each other. If numbers don't match (which is most likely to happen), then the developer with highest Story Point estimate will provide his assumptions for the estimate. Similarly, the developer with lowest Story Point estimate will provide a justification for his or her relative estimate. The team will engage in a focused discussion to understand the assumptions and risks. The process is repeated until a consensus is reached. Everyone must align to a specific Story Point estimate for a Product Backlog Item. This technique allows the team to provide mutually aligned estimates to each of the Product Backlog Items.

Next, let's discuss a technique to estimate the number of User Stories that form a Sprint Backlog and learn how to estimate the Sprint Backlog Items or Sprintable User Stories.

During Spring Planning meeting, the Development Team determines its capacity for the current Sprint. This is measured either as the number of Story Points that the team can accomplish in a Sprint or the number of available hours to perform the tasks. Next, they refer to the prioritized and estimated Product Backlog Items, and pick-up the PBIs that can fit into their available capacity for the Sprint.

To calculate the available capacity in terms of Story Points, the team refers to their past velocity or the Story Points that they accomplished in the last Sprint. For example, if the past velocity of the team was 20 Story Points and a member is taking time off for the upcoming Sprint, then the team's available capacity for the upcoming Sprint will be much less than 20 Story Points. Considering team size of 5 developers where each developer completed 4 Story Points in the previous Sprint, the available team capacity for the upcoming Sprint will be 16 Story Points.

To calculate the available team capacity in terms of hours for a two-week Sprint, the team accepts that they do not have complete ten days for development. Out of ten days, about a day's time is reserved for Scrum ceremonies such as Product Backlog Grooming, Sprint Planning, Sprint Review, and Sprint Retrospective. The team determines how much time should be reserved for work outside the Sprint such as production fixes, sizing new requests, team building activities, trainings, innovation workshops etc. Next, the team accounts for the time required to respond to daily emails, attend meetings, lunch breaks etc. The team also needs to know any planned vacation or scheduled time-off by any member during the Sprint. The time required for Scrum ceremonies, work outside the Sprint, meetings, breaks, and vacation is then subtracted from the total duration of ten days. Some teams also consider an additional buffer or contingency when calculating their available capacity.

Once the team determines its available capacity for the upcoming Sprint, it discusses the prioritized Product Backlog Items and their estimates to align on the number of User Stories that can be completed in the upcoming Sprint. For example, if the team's capacity is 16 Story Points, the first prioritized story is estimated for 5 Story Points, the second prioritized story is estimated for 1 Story Point, the third prioritized story is estimated for 3 Story Points, the fourth prioritized story is estimated for 3 Story Points, and the fifth prioritized story is estimated for 4 Story Points, then these top 5 User Stories will become part of the Sprint Backlog.

During Sprint Planning, the team also breaks down the Sprintable User Stories into detailed tasks, and then estimate each task in terms of the effort or hours required to complete the task. The team then validates the total task hours against their available capacity in hours to confirm the stories in the Sprint Backlog. For example, if the total estimate for all the detailed tasks in the Sprint Backlog is 400 hours, and if the available capacity for a five-member team is 300 hours, then it is likely that some of the User Stories will move back to the Product Backlog to be considered for the next Sprint.

Velocity

Velocity is the number of Story Points that the team delivers in one iteration or Sprint. So, if a Scrum team delivered User Stories worth 5 Story Points in one iteration, it means that their velocity for the Sprint is 5 points.

Velocity is used during initial planning, often called release planning to estimate the number of Sprints necessary for a release. For example, if there is a Product Backlog which is roughly estimated for 500 Story Points, and if the team's average velocity is around 50 Story Points, then we can estimate about 10 Sprints necessary for this release. We divide the total backlog size with the team's average velocity to determine the number of Sprints required for the release. Another approach is to use the team's highest velocity and the team's lowest velocity to come up with a range of Sprints necessary to complete a release. For example, if the high velocity is 50 Story Points, and the low velocity is 35 Story Points, then the 500-point backlog can be estimated to need around 10-14 Sprints to complete.

As learnt earlier, velocity is also used to determine the Stories that the Scrum team can commit to work in the upcoming Sprint. If a

Product Backlog has 50 User Stories, out of which 10 User Stories have been prioritized and sized during the Product Backlog Grooming meeting, and if the team's average velocity and their available capacity is say 8 Story Points, then they can only commit to complete the top prioritized stories with a total estimate of 8 Story Points.

The problem comes when the team doesn't know its velocity. If it's a new team, then they don't have a previous Sprint velocity for estimating their capacity in Story Points, or estimating the number of Sprints required for a release, or estimating the number of User Stories that they can commit to complete in the upcoming Sprint. In such cases, the team forecasts their velocity. During their first Sprint Planning meeting, they use their best judgement to decide how many User Stories they can complete within the upcoming Sprint. The total estimated size of the committed stories become the forecasted velocity for the team. Later, when the team completes the Sprint, the total Story Points of all the completed stories during the Sprint becomes their actual velocity for that Sprint.

Velocity Vs Productivity

First, we should understand that velocity is not same as productivity. Velocity is a measure to estimate work for the team. It is expressed in terms of average story points per Sprint. Productivity, on the other hand, is the number of units completed per unit of effort expended. It is typically expressed in terms of function points per person month or lines of code per person hour.

A team will high velocity does not mean that they are highly productive and vice versa. Velocity should never be used to evaluate the performance of the team. Many leaders struggle with ways to improve team's velocity. They fail to understand that having a consistent velocity is more important than having a high velocity. Next, I will explain few techniques to maintain a consistent team's velocity or to improve team's productivity:

Groom the stories for next two Sprints:
If a Scrum team participates in Product Backlog Grooming meetings during the Sprint to ensure that next two Sprint stories are refined and estimated, then the team will be aware of any impediments or roadblocks ahead of time and

the Sprint Planning meetings will go much faster. This also gives an opportunity for the Scrum team to provide their inputs on the sequence of the work and suggest ways to optimize the order of the stories. Understanding the potential roadblocks in advance enables the team to mitigate the same. Thus, grooming of stories two Sprints in advance help maintain a consistent team's velocity.

Conduct effective Sprint Retrospective meetings

Sprint Retrospective meetings provide an opportunity for the team to express their pain points in an open atmosphere. These meetings are conducted to identify process improvement ideas that can improve the productivity of the team or help the team to maintain a constant velocity for upcoming Sprints. For example, if the team could not deliver all the committed stories due to instability with their build environment, then the Scrum Master will initiate discussions with his or her peer Scrum Masters or senior leadership to create a stable build environment for the team.

Reduce accrual of Technical Debt

As learnt earlier, technical debt can lead to increased time to delivery. Technical debt can also lead to increased defects in the code which can cause frustration in the Scrum team. This frustration results in frequent interruptions, negative discussions, and team changes. People start pointing fingers at each other. Such an environment eventually impacts the productivity of the team, and decreases their average velocity. Thus, reducing the accrual of technical debt will result in a high performing and motivated team, and will ensure a consistent velocity.

Summary

In this chapter, I described the need for estimation along with the estimation units used for Scrum efforts. I also explained the Planning Poker technique to estimate the Product Backlog Items. Next, I focused on calculating capacity of a team in terms of both Story Points and person hours. I also described how to leverage the available capacity during Sprint Planning meeting. Then, I emphasized on velocity and how it is used. I also described the difference between velocity and productivity along with few techniques to maintain a consistent velocity. In the next chapter, I will explain the different charts used to communicate team's progress with stakeholders.

Chapter 11 – Communication

Most teams use a combination of charts to communicate their progress with other stakeholders. It is very important to publish the charts at regular intervals to create an environment of transparency and trust. There are a variety of graphs and charts that are common. The most commonly used are Release Burndown, Release Burnup, Sprint Burndown, Sprint Burnup, Velocity Chart, and Kanban Board. Let's look at each of these charts in detail.

Release Burndown Chart

For a fixed scope release, we communicate the team's progress using a burndown chart that shows the total amount of Story Points remaining at the end of each Sprint. The horizontal axis represents the number of Sprints within a release. The vertical axis represents the remaining Story Points.

The below table (Fig. 15) indicates the number of Story Points remaining at the end of each Sprint for a sample Release Burndown chart. The data is updated at the end of each Sprint to reflect the number of Story Points remaining for the release. As you see, at the end of first Sprint, the remaining stories were worth 95 Story Points. Again, at the end of second Sprint, the remaining Story Points for this release were 80. This implies that a total of 15 Story Points got completed during the second Sprint. This becomes the velocity for the second Sprint. Similarly, for the third Sprint, the number of completed Story Points is 10, hence the velocity for the third Sprint is 10 Story Points, and so on.

Sprints within a release	Remaining Story Points at the end of a Sprint
1	95
2	80
3	70
4	55
5	45
6	30
7	20
8	10
9	0

Fig. 15: Release Burndown Chart – Sample Data Table

Using this data, the Scrum Master creates a Release Burndown chart (see Fig. 16). This chart is primarily used to communicate the team's progress at the end of each Sprint. It is also used to predict or forecast the number of Sprints required at a given time to complete the remaining Story Points for a release. The team uses their highest, lowest, and average velocity to derive an optimistic, pessimistic, and the most likely forecast for the number of Sprints required to complete the remaining work. For example, at the end of third Sprint, when remaining Story Points are 70, highest team's velocity is 15, lowest team velocity is 10, and average team velocity is 12.5, the optimistic estimate for the number of Sprints required to complete the remaining work is 5, the pessimistic estimate is 7, and the most likely estimate is 6 more Sprints.

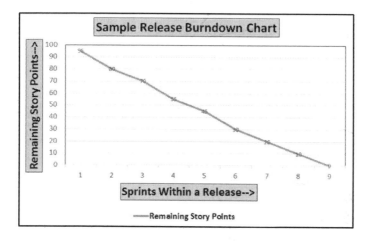

Fig. 16: Sample Release Burndown Chart

Another variation is a Release Burndown chart for a fixed date release. With a fixed date release, the total number of Sprints are fixed. This chart is used to communicate the Story Points completed at the end of each Sprint and to forecast the features that may be completed during the fixed duration.

Release Burnup Chart

For a fixed scope release, the Release Burnup chart depicts team's progress in terms of total amount of Story Points completed at the end of each Sprint. The total amount of work or Story Points for a release is shown as a target line on the chart. The horizontal axis represents the number of Sprints within a release. The vertical axis represents the completed Story Points.

The below table (Fig. 17) indicates the number of completed Story Points at the end of each Sprint for a sample Release Burnup chart. From the table, you can see that 10 Story Points were completed at the end of first Sprint, another 10 Story Points or total of 20 Story Points were completed at the end of second Sprint, a total of 35 Story Points were completed at the end of third Sprint, and so on.

Sprints within a release	Completed Story Points at the end of a Sprint
1	10
2	20
3	35
4	45
5	60
6	70
7	80
8	90
9	100

Fig. 17: Release Burnup Chart – Sample Data Table

Using this data, the Scrum Master creates a Release Burnup chart (see Fig. 18). This chart is primarily used to communicate the team's progress at the end of each Sprint. It is also used to predict the number of Sprints required at a given time to complete the total or target Story Points for a release. Like Release Burndown chart, the team determines an optimistic, pessimistic, and most likely estimate of the number of Sprints required to deliver the total Story Points for the release. In this example, the target line is at 100 Story Points, completed Story Points at the end of third Sprint are 35, highest team's velocity is 15, lowest team velocity is 10, average team velocity is 12.5, the optimistic estimate for the number of Sprints required to complete the target work is about 5 Sprints, the pessimistic estimate is about 7, and the most likely estimate is about 6 more Sprints.

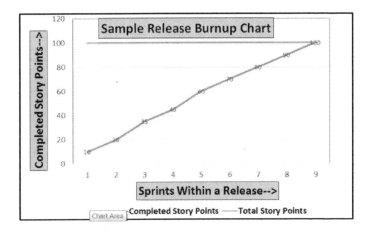

Fig. 18: Sample Release Burnup Chart

Sprint Burndown Chart

The Sprint Burndown or the Iteration Burndown chart is another powerful tool to communicate daily progress to the stakeholders. It tracks the completion of work for a given Sprint or an iteration. The horizontal axis represents the days within a Sprint. The vertical axis represents the hours remaining to complete the committed work.

The below table (Fig. 19) shows the number of hours remaining at the end of each day within a Sprint to create a sample Sprint Burndown chart. The ideal remaining hours are calculated by assuming a uniform rate of task completion each day.

Date	Ideal Remaining Effort (Hours)	Actual Remaining Effort (Hours)
3/15/16	180	180
3/16/16	160	170
3/17/16	140	155
3/18/16	120	140
3/21/16	100	125
3/22/16	80	100
3/23/16	60	70
3/24/16	40	50
3/25/16	20	25
3/28/16	0	0

**Fig. 19: Sprint Burndown Chart
– Sample Data Table**

The Scrum Master creates a Sprint Burndown chart using such data. The below diagram (see Fig. 20) depicts a sample Sprint Burndown chart with 'Date' represented on the horizontal axis and 'Remaining Effort (Hours)' represented on the vertical axis.

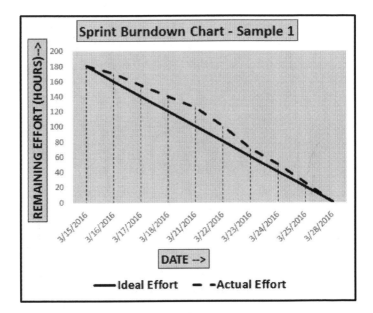

Fig. 20: Sprint Burndown Chart – Sample 1

In Fig. 20, the ideal effort is represented by a solid line, depicting the remaining effort at the start of the Sprint on 3/15/2016 as 180 hours, which then reduced to 160 hours on 3/16/2016, 140 hours on 3/17/2016 and so on, resulting in 0 hours on 3/28/2016. The ideal effort also assumes that all the planned work will be completed within the Sprint. That's why you see the solid line touching the horizontal axis at the end of the iteration i.e. on 3/28. However, this is seldom the case. In the above chart (see Fig. 20), the actual effort is represented by the dotted line. As the graph shows, the work was being done at a slower rate in the beginning. Later, the work was accelerated to complete within the Sprint.

Let's look at a second sample Sprint Burndown chart in Fig. 21. Here again, the actual effort is represented by the dotted line. Did you notice the difference between the two charts? In the second chart, the dotted line does not touch the horizontal axis at the end of the Sprint, which signifies that the team was not able to complete all the committed work for that Sprint. In such scenarios, the unfinished work at the end of the Sprint moves back to the Product Backlog and then gets reprioritized to be picked up in the next Sprint.

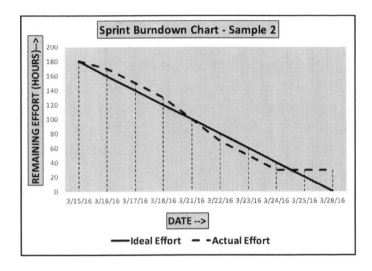

Fig. 21: Sprint Burndown Chart – Sample 2

Sprint Burnup Chart

The Sprint Burnup or the Iteration Burnup chart is an alternative way to visualize progress within a Sprint. The horizontal axis represents the days within a Sprint, whereas the vertical axis represents the completed Story Points or the completed hours during a Sprint. This chart looks like a Release Burnup chart; the difference is that the Release Burnup chart represents the work completed in a release, while the Sprint Burnup chart represents the work completed in a Sprint.

The below table (Fig. 22) indicates the number of completed Story Points at the end of each day within a Sprint.

Days within a Sprint	Completed Story Points
1	1
2	3
3	4
4	6
5	7
6	9
7	10
8	11
9	13
10	15

Fig. 22: Sprint Burnup Chart – Sample Data Table

This data is leveraged to create a Sprint Burnup chart (see Fig. 23) which is an alternative visual way to track and communicate daily progress of a Scrum team. It depicts the rate of Story Points completion during a Sprint.

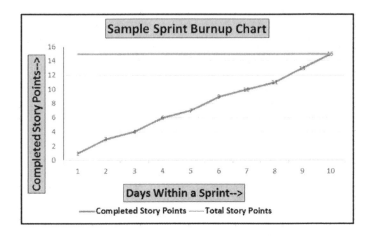

Fig. 23: Sample Sprint Burnup Chart

Velocity Chart

Velocity is the average amount of work that the Development Team completes within one iteration or Sprint. This is usually measured in terms of Story Points. It is the number of Story Points that were accepted during the iteration. Velocity is useful in estimating the number of Sprints required to complete the sized work in the Product Backlog. For example, if the backlog items are sized for a total of 100 Story Points, and if the Scrum team has an average Velocity of 20 Story Points, then we can assume that the team may take approximately 5 Sprints to complete the sized backlog items.

The below table (Fig. 24) indicates the team's velocity for each Sprint. From the table, you can see that the team had a velocity of 20 Story Points during Iteration 22, a velocity of 35 Story Points during Iteration 23, and so on.

Iterations	Velocity (accepted story points)
Iteration 22	20
Iteration 23	35
Iteration 24	25
Iteration 25	15
Iteration 26	10
Iteration 27	30
Iteration 28	25

Fig. 24: Velocity Chart
– Sample Data Table

A sample Velocity chart is depicted in the below diagram (see Fig. 25) where 'Iterations' are represented on the horizontal axis, and 'Velocity' is represented on the vertical axis. The stakeholders leverage this chart to understand the average velocity of a team and to estimate the duration required by the team to complete a release. In this example, the maximum velocity for the team was 35 Story Points, the minimum velocity was 10 Story Points, and thus, the average velocity of this team was calculated to be about 22.85 Story Points.

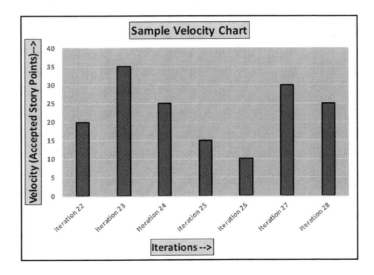

Fig. 25: Sample Velocity Chart

Kanban or a Task Board

This is one of the most simple and powerful ways to communicate progress of the team. It provides a quick visual representation to team's progress during a Sprint. A Kanban board has three main columns – Tasks to do, Tasks in progress, and Tasks completed. When a Sprint starts, all the committed tasks appear in 'Tasks to do' column. The team then selects the tasks that they want to start first, and move them to 'Tasks in progress' column. When a task is complete, it is moved into 'Tasks Completed' column.

The Kanban board can be customized to add additional columns to visualize the flow of work at different stages. Some teams prefer to add columns such as Tasks Tested, Tasks Blocked, etc. The below diagram (Fig. 26) shows a sample Kanban board for two User Stories being worked upon by a Scrum team. This board gives a quick visual representation of the status of each task associated with the User Stories that the team is working on. The team updates the board regularly to depict the latest status as much as possible.

User Stories	Tasks to do	Tasks in progress	Tasks Completed
US01	Build the validation logic	Add new fields	HTML mockup
	Add Alt Text to images	Create new images	
US02	Display transactions	Retrieve data from the web service	Data mapping
	Build the search functionality	Create a widget	

Fig. 26: Sample Kanban Board

Summary

In this chapter, I described the different charts that are commonly used to communicate team's progress to product stakeholders. First, I explained Release Burndown charts that show the total amount of Story Points remaining at the end of each Sprint. I also created a sample data table and then leveraged that data to create a sample chart. Next, I focused on Release Burnup charts that show the total amount of Story Points completed at the end of each

Sprint. I also emphasized on Sprint Burndown and Sprint Burnup charts that are used to communicate progress during a Sprint. Next, I described Velocity Chart that is used to communicate team's velocity across the Sprints. Finally, I highlighted the usage of a task board or a Kanban board which represents the current state of tasks within a Sprint.

Chapter 12 – Resources

In the earlier chapters, I have explained the Scrum framework. You should now understand the Scrum approach, and the benefits it has over the plan-driven sequential development approach. You should now be aware of the Scrum roles, ceremonies, artifacts, principles, and rules. You should also now understand the mechanics of a Sprint, how to create User Stories, and how to minimize Technical Debt. You also understand the different estimation techniques, velocity, and progress charts.

Next, you must discover your best approach based on your organization's goals and environment. No matter what the situation is, whether you are new to Scrum or are already using Scrum, you can use its principles to guide you forward. When applying Scrum, you should learn, inspect, and adapt with each Sprint. Scrum is all about continuous learning and continuous improvement.

I will now provide some additional resources to learn more about Scrum. I will also list the different Scrum certifications that you can take to enhance your career growth.

Useful Websites

- www.scrum.org
- www.scrumalliance.org
- www.mountaingoatsoftware.com
- https://en.wikipedia.org/wiki/Scrum_(software_development)
- http://www.scrumhub.com
- http://reqtest.com/agile-blog/15-awesome-free-resources-to-learn-more-about-agile-and-scrum-methodology/
- http://www.scrumguides.org
- http://scrummethodology.com
- http://www.scaledagileframework.com

Scrum Certifications

Scrum alliance provides certifications for Scrum practitioners as listed below:

- Certified Scrum Master (CSM)
- Certified Scrum Product Owner (CSPO)
- Certified Scrum Developer (CSD)
- Certified Scrum Professional (CSP)

You may check out their below link:
https://www.scrumalliance.org/certifications

Scrum.Org also provides Scrum assessments and certifications as listed below:

- Professional Scrum Master (PSM)
- Professional Scrum Product Owner (PSPO)
- Professional Scrum Developer (PSD)

You may check out their below link:
https://www.scrum.org/Assessments/Scrumorg-Certifications

Summary

In this chapter, I provided some useful websites and list of certifications to pursue your learning further. I hope you have enjoyed this book.

Bibliography

Rubin, Kenneth S. Essential Scrum: A Practical Guide to the Most Popular Agile Process. Michigan: Addison-Wesley, July 2012

Schwaber, Ken, and Sutherland, Jeff. "Scrum Guide." scrumguides. 2010 http://www.scrumguides.org/

Ocamb, Scott. "What does the Agile Manifesto Mean?." Scrum Alliance. 24 Apr 2013 https://www.scrumalliance.org/community/articles/2013/2013-april/what-does-the-agile-manifesto-mean

Post your review!

Self-published authors completely rely on feedback from their readers. Please submit your honest review on Amazon. Thanks for your support!

82651898R00084

Made in the USA
Middletown, DE
04 August 2018